Revised Edition

Failure Reporting, Analysis, and Corrective Action System

RICKY SMITH • BILL KEETER

An Easy-to-Use System to Improve Maintenance Reliability

FRACAS
Failure Reporting, Analysis, and Corrective Action System

Revised Edition

By Ricky Smith and Bill Keeter

ISBN
978-0-9820517-6-4
HF072015

© Copyright 2015 Reliabilityweb.com.
First Published in 2011.

All rights reserved.
Printed in United States of America

This book, or any parts thereof, may not be reproduced,
stored in a retrieval system, or transmitted in any form
without the permission of the Publisher.

Opinions expressed in this book are solely the authors and
do not necessarily reflect the views of the Publisher.

Publisher's Disclaimer:
The authors of this book have gratefully used
contributions from the research and work of many industry experts.
Vigilant efforts have been made to properly credit the work
within and to ensure the accuracy of the content.
Reliabilityweb.com shall not be held liable for any
inaccuracies or oversights in these credits.

Publisher: Terrence O'Hanlon
Cover and Book Design: Nicola Behr

For information: Reliabilityweb.com
www.reliabilityweb.com
8991 Daniels Center Dr., Suite #105
Fort Myers, FL 33912
Toll Free: 888-575-1245, Office: 239-333-2500
E-mail: customerservice@reliabilityweb.com

10   9   8   7

INTRODUCTION

Why FRACAS?

This book was written based on the knowledge that most companies cannot and do not perform an effective failure identification, analysis, and corrective action system and thus spend a lot of time and money chasing what they consider "bad actors." FRACAS is the best method for continuous improvement of your maintenance strategy through the use of good failure data, accurate analysis, and implementation of an effective corrective action. The corrective action could come in the form of a maintenance strategy adjustment or a redesign. Most people do not understand the power of FRACAS, and in this book we will unlock this awesome tool and change the way you view failures.

This book can help any company be successful at failure elimination. The only ingredient you will need to add will be "discipline" to ensure everyone follows the program so that the full benefits can be found in lower cost, higher availability, lower replacement cost, and fewer chances of an unknown failure.

ACKNOWLEDGMENTS

This was written with assistance and dedication from some of the best maintenance and reliability professionals in the business. They must be named, even if they do not want to accept credit for their contribution: John Schultz, Andy Page, Doug Plucknette, Mike Gehloff, Walter Neijsen, Tim Goshert, and Terrence O'Hanlon. Without the help of Terrence and the Board of Directors at GPAllied this book would not be possible. Reliabilityweb.com has been a great place to learn and inspired us to write this book.

We would also like to thank the Society for Maintenance and Reliability Professionals for their inspiration and guidance in the maintenance and reliability community worldwide.

TABLE OF CONTENTS

Chapter 1: What is FRACAS and Failure Reporting? 1
    What is FRACAS and Failure Reporting? 1
    Failure Reporting Questionnaire 2
    The Cost of Failures 3
    Requirements for Failure Reporting 6

Chapter 2: The Basics of Failures 13
    What is a Failure? 13
    Failure Patterns 15
    Causes of Failures 17
    Hidden Failures 18
    Threads Between Common Failures 19

Chapter 3: Eliminating Failures (Can it be done?) 21
    Do I Need to Eliminate All Failures? 21
    Consequence, Risk, and Criticality 22
    Managing Failures versus Eliminating Failures 23
    How the U.S. Navy Began Eliminating
    Infant Failures 25
    The Evolution of Maintenance 26
    The Evolution of Maintenance in the U.S. Navy 27
    State of Manufacturing 28

Chapter 4: Understanding FRACAS in Simple Terms 31
    Defining the Terms 31

Types of Failure Reporting 33
    Crisis Failures 33
    Chronic Failures 34
Types of Failure Analysis... 35
Statistical Analysis Methods 36
    1. Pareto Analysis 36
    2. Weibull Analysis... 37
Failure Elimination Analysis.. 38
    Root Cause Analysis 38
    Corrective Action Selection................................ 39

Chapter 5: Failure Reports 43
Failure Reporting 44
Failure Report Examples... 44
Asset Health or Percent of Assets with
No Identifiable Defects 44
    2. Mean Time Between Failures, Mean Time To Repairs, and Mean Time Between Repairs 45
    3. Mean Time Between Failure by Plant, Area, System, and Equipment Type 46
    4. Cost Variance by Area of the Plant................... 46
    5. Most Frequent Part-Defect-Cause Report 47
    6. Most Dominant Failure Pattern Identification.. 47

Chapter 6: Weibull Analysis (Everything you wanted to know but were afraid to ask) 51
Introduction to Weibull Analysis 51
The Bathtub Curve 52
What Do Beta Values Tell Us?.................................... 53
Infant Failure... 53
High Failure Rate Random Failures 55
Short Life Wear-out Failures (Early Wear-out)........... 56

      How Do I Know What I Have?
      (How to build Weibull shapes with no data)............... 57
      Changing the Failure Mechanisms............................. 59

Chapter 7: Steps to Implementing an Effective FRACAS........ 63
      FRACAS Checklist... 63
      5 Steps to Building a Failure
      Elimination/Mitigation Program...................................... 64
          1. Effective Equipment Hierarchy........................ 64
          2. Asset Criticality Analysis................................. 65
          3. Identification of Failure Modes....................... 69
          4. Develop a Maintenance Strategy..................... 70
          5. Executing the Proactive Work from
          the Maintenance Strategies............................... 77

Chapter 8: The Cost of Unreliability 89
      The Market Survivor Model 90
      Example Number One of Unreliability 91
      Example Number Two of Unreliability –
      Different Context 91
      Maintenance Cost Reduction 92
      Building a Reliable Organization................................... 93
      Managing Reliability or Asset Health........................... 94
      Nowlan and Heap Report on Reliability 97

**Chapter 9: Managing Change in a Failure Elimination
          Organization 99**
      The Proactive Organization and Failure Elimination ... 99
      Characteristics of a Proactive Organization 100
      Discipline 101
      Discipline and Failure Elimination 102
      Implementing Discipline..103

Chapter 10: 107

    Seven Steps to a Working FRACAS 107

    Sustainable Change Is the Objective 107

    FRACAS Step 1 – Determine Your End Goal 109

    FRACAS Step 2 – Create the Data Collection Plan ... 109

    FRACAS Step 3 – Determine Organizational Roles, Goals, and Responsibilities (RACI) 112

    FRACAS Step 4 – Create the FRACAS Policies and Procedures Manual 113

    FRACAS Step 5 – Develop and Execute the FRACAS Training Plan 114

    FRACAS Step 6 – Implement the FRACAS 115

    FRACAS Step 7 – Monitor and Adjust 116

Addendum: 117

    True Failure Experiences 117

        1. Failure: Partial Functional Failure Leads to Total Functional Failure 117

        2. Failure: Gearbox Input Shaft Bearing Failure 118

    Help Documents 123

        Accurate Work Order Close Out 123

        Key Definitions 125

        Failure Collection Series 128

        Potential Failures 130

About the Authors: 135

CHAPTER 1

What is FRACAS and Failure Reporting?

"Your system is perfectly designed to give you the results that you get."
- W. Edwards Deming, PhD

What is FRACAS and Failure Reporting?

FRACAS (Failure Reporting, Analysis, and Corrective Action System) provides the process by which failures can be reported in a timely manner, analyzed, and a corrective action system put into place in order to eliminate or mitigate the recurrence of a failure.

During a recent poll, not one company felt they had an effective failure reporting system. The main problem found was threefold:

1. **Not knowing which failure reports were needed and when.** Before we start a journey, we must know where we are going.

2. **Not having data in the CMMS/EAM to help with failure reporting.** Once we know where we are going we must then develop the data input to provide us with the reporting output. Then, the hardest part is to ensure people input the correct data into the correct data field. As you have been told, trash in = trash out.

3. **No one clearly responsible for managing the FRACAS process at any level.** Everyone seems to dodge the bullet when it comes to reporting failure, analyzing the data, and taking corrective action. I have seen many companies who do a great job of going after a large failure (one occurrence) with Root Cause Analysis (RCA), but what amazes me is they do not implement the recommendations fast enough. The other problem is that most large failures are truly caused by small component failures which could have been predicted or prevented. Not all, but most.

The poll results should not come as a shock to anyone, so ask yourself, "How good is our organization at identifying failures?" Sure, you see a failure when it occurs, but can you identify when equipment reliability is having serious problems? Most companies begin applying RCA (Root Cause Analysis) or RCFA (Root Cause Failure Analysis) to "high value failures" which is not wrong, but I prefer to not see a failure, or to eliminate failures to a controllable level.

During the FRACAS process, the reports acquired from the CMMS/EAM or other specialized Reliability Software are analyzed with the objective being to eliminate, mitigate, or control failures. These reports could include Cost Variance, Mean Time Between Failure (MTBF), Mean Time Between Repair (MTBR), Dominant Failure Patterns in your operation, or common threads between failures such as "lack of lubrication" due to the lubricator not using known industry standards. Do not think that everyone has this process working great for them. The goal of this book is to help you better understand failures and the reporting required to eliminate or control the failures that are killing reliability in most organizations.

Failure Reporting Questionnaire

Let's answer these simple questions to see where you stand with failure reporting. Answer them honestly to see if you have any problems with identifying failures and effectively eliminating or mitigating their effects on Total Process and Asset Reliability:

1. Can you identify the top ten assets which had the most losses due to a partial or total functional failure by running a report on your maintenance software?
2. Can you identify the total process and asset losses in an organization for the past 365 days?
3. Can you identify components with a common thread due to a specific failure pattern, as shown in Figure 1-1?

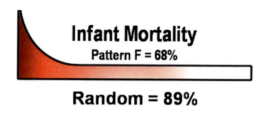

Figure 1-1: Failure Pattern (Nowlan and Heap)

The Cost of Failures

> **Functional Failure:** A state in which the physical asset or system is unable to perform a specific function to a level of performance that is acceptable by its owner or user. Functional failure can be either a total or partial loss of function. *Example:* A 40 GPM pump is no longer pumping 40 GPM or transferring product. (It is down because of some type of failure mode or modes.)

Generally speaking, companies understand the costs associated with equipment breakdowns. Breakdowns are very obvious because they result not only in the loss of function of the individual component, but also in the loss of function of the entire system. The costs of functional failures that result in partial loss of system function are not so easy to understand, and are commonly called hidden losses. In this section we will discuss various types of functional failures and their causes. At the end of the section we will look at a type of production plot that allows an organization to quantify both partial and total loss of system function so that their costs can be equally understood.

FRACAS

Functional Failure Category	Failure Type	Causes	Cost Category
Total	Equipment breakdown	• Ineffective repair, preventive maintenance, lubrication, and predictive maintenance procedures	Visible
	Premature or infant equipment failures (Shown to be a major cause of business losses)	• Improper operation • Ineffective or nonexistent commissioning procedures* • Preventive and Predictive Maintenance tasks not directed at specific failure modes • Best known maintenance repair and installation practices not being followed	
Partial	Equipment operating below maximum effective rate	• Ineffective or nonexistent operating procedures • Inadequate operator training • Management not aware of maximum effective rate	Often Hidden
Partial/ Total	Off-quality product misidentified as first-pass quality (This is a case where quality losses aren't counted because the material can be reworked into first quality product.)	• Acceptance of rework as a way of managing final quality.	Often Hidden

*Effective commissioning procedures allow organizations to prevent or find installation defects that could result in premature or infant failures. Figures 1-2 and 1-3 are examples of installation defects found using Thermography.

Figures 1-2 and 1-3: Defects Identified

In the 1990s, Paul Barringer invented a unique plot called the Process Reliability (PR) Plot. The value of the PR Plot is that it manipulates production data in a way that allows organizations to quantify losses based on whether they are a part of normal process variation, or an extreme loss of reliability.

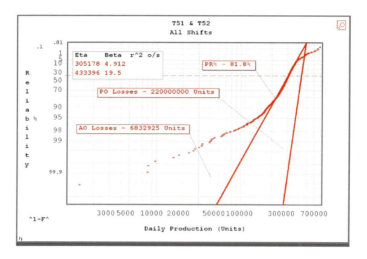

Figure 1-4: Process Reliability Plot Showing Failure Losses

Keeping it simple: A process reliability plot can determine the split between maintenance and process losses.

Table 1-1: Process Reliability Plot Loss Characterization

Loss Category	Causes	Percentage of Total Losses
PO (Process Optimization)	• Equipment operating below maximum rate • Lack of "Operating Discipline" • Off-quality product • Short and frequent equipment stoppages	97%
AO (Availability Optimization)	• Long equipment breakdowns • Long periods of planned maintenance for PMs • No production due to lack of sales	3%

FRACAS

The problem for many organizations is that PO type losses are often hidden. In fact these losses are often referred to as the hidden factory. In less well-run organizations, the variation associated with PO losses is frequently viewed as "That's just the way things work around here." From a practical viewpoint PO losses are generally reduced by Lean/Six Sigma Efforts, and AO losses are generally reduced by optimizing equipment maintenance strategies and aggressive sales and marketing. PO losses are said to be "management issues" because reducing them usually requires a significant amount of management attention.

Requirements for Failure Reporting

Eliminating failures requires an organization to move from a "reactive" to a "proactive" maintenance model (Figures 1-5 and 1-6). This requires the organization to follow **"Known Best Practices"** in maintenance.

These are requirements of a successful Failure Reporting, Analysis, and Corrective Action System:

1. Failure data is collected, analyzed, and disseminated in your CMMS/EAM.
2. Preventive and Predictive Maintenance plans are developed based on known failure modes and/or regulatory compliance.
3. Planners do not become involved in emergency or urgent work.
4. Parts are kitted for planned jobs.
5. Effective/repeatable work procedures are developed and followed for all corrective, preventive, lubrication, and predictive maintenance tasks.
6. Maintenance scheduling is managed by the day and reported by the week.
7. Key performance indicators are used to measure performance of each function in the maintenance process (Proactive Work Flow Model).

You may have a proactive maintenance process, however, if you do not have the discipline to follow the process, failures will continue to occur even if you implement the best failure reporting system in the world. You will find you're chasing failures all the time. "Perform Root Cause Analysis" becomes a statement no one believes will bring any tangible benefits, especially if the organization is reactive and not disciplined.

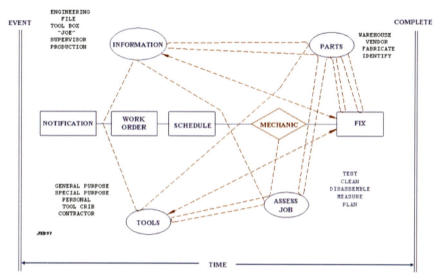

Figure 1-5: Reactive Maintenance Model

Figure 1-5 is a great example of what reactive organizations use as their default maintenance model. An emergency occurs and the maintenance staff (and not the maintenance planner) responds by identifying parts, tools, etc., while precious time and production is lost. The question after the repair is completed may be: "How long before this failure occurs again?" The answer is: "We do not know if an effective failure reporting system is in place." Until an organization can follow a Proactive Work Flow Model, I would not attempt FRACAS. You must have a process by which continuous improvement is in place and followed.

Table 1-2 will help you to better identify whether your organization status is either reactive or proactive. You can only be one, is the rule. We may not like the rule, but rules are to ensure we have true alignment in our thinking and actions.

FRACAS

Table 1-2: Reactive or Emergency Maintenance vs. Proactive Maintenance

Emergency Maintenance Means:	Proactive Maintenance Means:
Late detection by operators	Early detection by skilled maintenance technicians using advanced monitoring technologies
Waiting for things to happen	Thinking about things before they happen. Identifying problems that are still small and easy to fix
Immediate shutdowns and indefinite downtime	Planned, scheduled shutdowns to keep downtime to a minimum
Expediting spare parts -- regardless of costs	Planning and ordering spare parts in advance
Working overtime, 24/7 until repairs are made	Having everything prepared for – scheduling maintenance crews to do the job right the first time
High costs	Low costs
High stress	Low stress
High safety risk	Low safety risk
Blame, finger-pointing, frustration, distrust, pessimism, waste	Confidence, pride, job security, teamwork, optimism, rewarding

Figure 1-6 shows a Proactive Work Flow Model, which many companies use; however, the part which is missing in most organizations is the FRACAS Loop which is the continuous improvement loop for reducing or eliminating failures through redesign or changes in maintenance strategy. FRACAS is defined as the process by which failure reports and data are analyzed so that corrective action can be taken to eliminate or mitigate a failure.

In the process of being proactive, an organization needs to include FRACAS in the proactive work flow process and understand how it benefits an organization. The goal is to eliminate or mitigate failures.

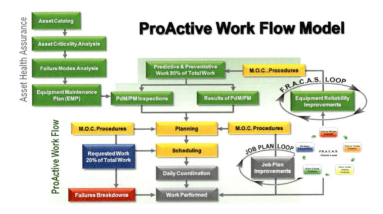

Figure 1-6: Proactive Work Flow Model

To make FRACAS a part of your continuous improvement process you must identify when total and partial functional failures occur so that someone (an operator or maintenance technician) can identify and record these failures correctly in your CMMS/EAM—yes, this should include partial and total functional failures from production. If the data is collected correctly, maintenance and reliability leaders can use FRACAS to make changes to their maintenance strategy which will make an impact on a large scale at first, and on a smaller scale as specific problem failure patterns are either eliminated or controlled. Production can use this data to support changes to operating procedures or process control parameters.

The foundational elements are keys to success because they assure asset health. These are requirements (not options) to ensure that you have a sustainable Proactive Work Flow Model. Reliability engineering many times identifies the wrong failure mode and thus the wrong Equipment Maintenance Plan (EMP) is implemented. FRACAS data analysis assists in making changes to a maintenance strategy, and thus the right failure modes are now addressed and can be prevented or predicted. Without all the elements of the Proactive Work Flow Model working effectively, continuous improvement will be a rare event. This may surprise you. If an organization's preventive maintenance and predictive maintenance programs are not developed based on the prevention or prediction of specific failure modes, then FRACAS will not be effective.

Remember, the objective of the Proactive Work Flow Model is to provide discipline and repeatability to your maintenance process. In addition, this model ensures that FRACAS will provide the continuous improvement for your maintenance strategies (see Figure 1-7). These are fundamental items you must have in place to ensure you receive the results you expect.

FRACAS

Figure 1-7: FRACAS Loop

Think of FRACAS in this manner: As you have failures using your codes in your CMMS/EAM, part-defect-cause is identified on failures on critical assets and you begin to make serious improvements in your operations reliability. Looking at the FRACAS Loop model above (Figure 1-7), we begin with work order history analysis and from this analysis we decide if we need to apply Root Cause Analysis (RCA) to eliminate failures on critical equipment. Reliability Centered Maintenance (RCM) and Failure Mode and Effect Analysis (FMEA) are two tools that can also be used with RCA to reduce or eliminate failures. From the RCA, we determine maintenance strategy adjustments needed to predict or prevent failures. After we make the strategy adjustments, we may find that new failure modes not covered by your strategy occur. You can now make a new failure code to track the new failure mode so additional failures can be tracked and managed when you review work order history. You can see this is a continuous improvement loop which never ends.

Chapter Summary

FRACAS provides the continuous improvement for any maintenance and reliability program. Its main focus is failure elimination through the use of maintenance failure data, not failure management. See the I-P-F Curve in Figure 1-8.

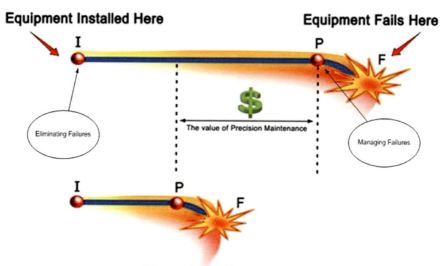

Figure 1-8: I-P-F Curve

References

Day, John, *Proactive Maintenance*, 1983, Republished in *Rules of Thumb for Maintenance and Reliability Engineers*, Elsevier Publishing, 2008.

Page, Andy, "Process Reliability Plot," GPAllied, 2008, np.

Page, Andy, "Modern Approach to Risk Management," Allied Reliability, 2007.

CHAPTER 2

The Basics of Failures

What is a Failure?

Almost every maintenance organization sets some sort of failure elimination goal. The problem is this goal is often set without fully understanding what a failure is. In some organizations, equipment isn't considered failed unless it is totally inoperative. In others, equipment is considered failed if there is some partial loss of function such as reduced production rate, or off-quality production outside their normal targets. There are constant arguments about whether there was ever really a failure. Eliminating failures requires a slightly different outlook on what constitutes a failure.

Let's begin by taking a look at the definition generated by Nowlan and Heap in their seminal work, *Reliability-Centered Maintenance* (Nowlan and Heap):

FRACAS

> "Without a precise definition of what condition represents a failure, there is no way to assess its consequences or to define the physical evidence for which to inspect. The term failure must, in fact, be given a far more explicit definition than 'an inability to function' in order to clarify the basis of Reliability-Centered Maintenance."

> "A failure is an unsatisfactory condition. In other words, a failure is an identifiable deviation from the original condition which is unsatisfactory to a particular user."

They further define two types of failures:

> "A functional failure is the inability of an item (or the equipment containing it) to meet a specified performance standard and is usually identified by an operator."

> "A potential failure is an identifiable physical condition which indicates a functional failure is imminent and is usually identified by a maintenance technician using predictive or quantitative preventive maintenance."

Predictive or condition-based maintenance is based on the concept that there is sufficient time between when the potential failure is detected and the functional failure occurs for the organization to react and prevent the functional failure. This interval is known as the P-F interval. Point P is the first detection of failure. Point F is the point at which failure occurs. If you had a disciplined failure elimination process the P-F interval could be identified; however, it is only possible for very few best practices companies. The P-F interval states that once point P is detected and you know F, you take half that amount of time and make the correction or replacement to the equipment. This concept could work if applied to time-based failures which are only 11% of failures, where 89% are random.

The Basics of Failures

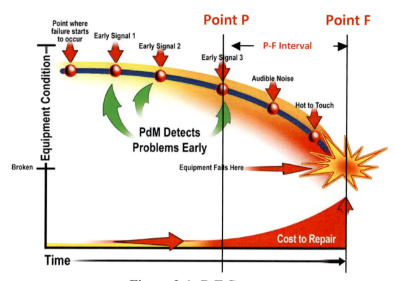

Figure 2-1: P-F Curve

These definitions mean that it is up to individual organizations to decide what constitutes an unacceptable condition. This decision significantly impacts whether or not an organization will actually be able to eliminate all functional failures except for those they have decided to accept. By making a run-to-failure, or no scheduled maintenance decision, management has made a risk-based decision to run the equipment until functional failure is reached.

Failure Patterns

Age and reliability studies conducted on aircraft components over a period of years revealed the six basic age-reliability relationships shown in Figure 2-2. The vertical axis of these curves represents the conditional probability of failure, and the horizontal axis represents time in service after installation or overhaul.

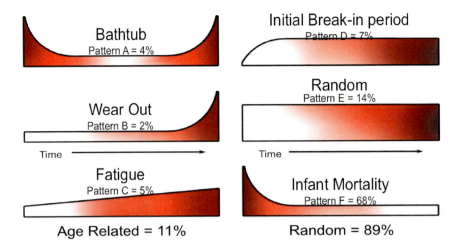

**Figure 2-2: Aircraft Component Failure Patterns
(Nowlan and Heap, John Moubray)**

What is particularly striking about these curves is the very low percentage of items that display a distinct wear-out region, the large number of items that display a random failure region, and the extremely high percentage of items that display an infant failure region. Only patterns A and B which represent only 6% of the items studied display the wear-out region denoted by a rapidly increasing conditional probability of failure at the right-hand end of the curve. Ninety-five percent of the items studied had at least some region of random failures denoted by a flat region in the curve. Pattern C was the only curve that did not have some region of random failure. *This means that 95% of the equipment in the study may benefit from some form of condition monitoring and only 6% may benefit from time-based replacement or overhaul.*

It is important to recognize the significance of pattern F, or Infant Mortality. Sixty-eight percent of the items studied had a high conditional probability of failure immediately after installation and commissioning. The majority of item failures were being induced by activities directly related to time-based replacements and overhauls. The overall maintenance strategy present at the time was extremely faulty, and was not achieving the desired goals of restoring, protecting, and preserving the function of the equipment in the safest, most economical manner.

Causes of Failures

All equipment failures are governed by the simple laws of physics present in everyday life. Friction, erosion, corrosion, stress, and impact are the physical basis for most failures. It is the interaction of humans with the equipment that determines whether these causes occur normally or abnormally.

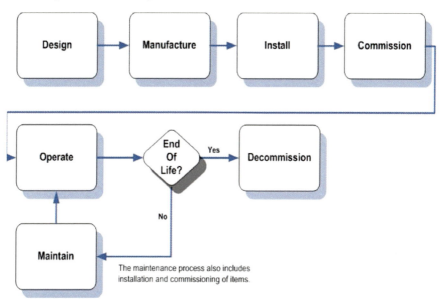

Figure 2-3: Equipment Item Life Cycle

As we can see in Figure 2-3, human interaction with the equipment occurs at every phase of an item's life. Substandard performance and errors at any phase will result in decreased reliability, and the result will be lower profits, more environmental incidents, and more safety incidents. In general, Preventive Maintenance (PM) activities are designed to either prevent the physical sources of failure from occurring, or to remove the item before degradation caused by those forces results in loss of equipment function. As we saw from the six failure shapes, there is a very small percentage of equipment that will benefit from time-based replacement or overhaul. A PM strategy is dependent on knowing which equipment has the wear-out pattern, and when the best time is to perform the PM.

A failure elimination strategy is driven by finding those actions that create random failures, infant failures, and early wear-out failures, and

FRACAS

eliminating them. The Failure Reporting, Analysis, and Corrective Action System (FRACAS) is designed to help the organization detect common failure modes, determine the causes of the failure modes, and eliminate them. Table 2-1 shows that stopping at the physical root of a failure will probably not eliminate future failures of the same type. The RCA absolutely has to address the human side of the failure equation.

Table 2-1: Sources of Failures

Source	Failure Characteristics
Design Errors	• Early wear-out • High frequency of random failures
Manufacturing Errors	• Infant failures
Installation Errors	• Infant failures
Commissioning Errors	• Infant failures
Operating Errors	• Infant failures • Early wear-out • Hi frequency of random failures
Maintenance Errors	• Infant failures • Early wear-out

Hidden Failures

Hidden failures are functional failures that share two very important characteristics. First, they can't be seen by the operators during normal operation of the system. Second, they are usually in items that protect people from severe injury or death, or protect equipment from severe damage. The combination of those two characteristics means that they must have some sort of hidden failure finding task assigned to them as part of any maintenance strategy. It is important to remember that the longer the hidden loss of function is present, the higher the risk of a catastrophic consequence.

Threads Between Common Failures

The failures we see in an organization are either crisis failures or chronic failures. Table 2-2 delineates the characteristics of the two types. The primary thing to remember is that solving chronic failures actually changes the system's overall output. The goal with FRACAS is to be able to recognize the chronic failures, determine and eliminate the cause, and spread that solution across the organization either nationally or internationally.

Table 2-2: Basic Functional Failure Types (Reliability Center)

Failure Type	Characteristics
Crisis	• Deviation from normal is sudden and severe • Usually demands immediate attention • Will bring to it whatever resources it needs to correct itself
Chronic	• Deviation from normal is not severe • Deviation is often viewed as a normal part of operations • Occurs routinely • Sneaks under the radar

In most instances crisis failures will be analyzed, and the root cause will be eliminated. With a good FRACAS, we will be able to see the commonality of failure modes that create chronic failures. We will be able to use the data to determine which of the failure patterns the failure modes fit and take appropriate action to eliminate them. The beauty of a well-defined corporate level FRACAS is that failures in every facility can be tracked, and failure modes that are common across the entire corporation can be addressed. That translates into substantial reductions in overall cost. You may find that a certain brand of pump suffers early seal failures in every facility that uses them regardless of

FRACAS

the quality of local repairs. Or you may find that facilities in a certain region are experiencing fewer failures, and a different failure pattern for the same failure mode. In any case, the failure patterns will be easier to determine because the significant failure modes have been recorded and analyzed using the proper tools.

Chapter Summary

In this chapter we have looked at a working definition of failure that allows organizations to decide for themselves what a failure is by defining which events are unsatisfactory. We saw how the definitions of potential and functional failure are related to condition monitoring. We looked at the six common failure patterns and saw from them that a large number of failures could benefit from condition monitoring, and that a large number of defects are actually induced in equipment by the actions of maintaining and commissioning the equipment. We also looked at how failures can be caused at every point in the life cycle of equipment starting in the design phase. The concept of crisis and chronic failures was introduced, and we looked at how a FRACAS can be used to ferret out chronic failures to help improve overall business performance.

In the next chapter, we will talk about eliminating failures. We will look at the I-P-F curve and see how it relates to eliminating versus managing failures, and then we'll look at how the U.S. Navy used the concept of procedures-based maintenance to significantly reduce infant failures.

References

Nowlan, F. Stanley, and Heap, Howard F.,
Reliability-Centered Maintenance, Department of
Defense Report Number A066-579, December 29, 1978.

*Failure Analysis/Problem-Solving Methods Student
Manual*, Reliability Center, Inc., nd.

CHAPTER 3

Eliminating Failures (Can it be done?)

Do I Need to Eliminate All Failures?

Nearly every time I have asked a maintenance manager if he had enough resources, the answer has been no. There never seems to be enough people, time, or money to achieve all the things an organization wants to accomplish. This lack of infinite resources means that we must have a reasonable way of managing a failure elimination program. The main thing we need to remember is that we want a management system that everyone in the organization can understand. We have to find some way to change "maintenance speak" to "management speak" so that management is on board with what we are trying to accomplish, and so they understand why we are doing it the way we are.

FRACAS

Consequence, Risk, and Criticality

Consequence is the business impact of a failure. Most failures have multiple consequences. Not all failures create the same business consequence so we must have some way to separate the business impact of individual failures. The way we do this is through a severity ranking matrix. Many businesses already have some sort of severity matrix for safety and environmental events. If yours does not have one, you will need to work with operations, safety, and environmental resources to develop one that all parties can agree to. Table 3-1 is a representative matrix that could be used as a starting point.

Table 3-1: Sample Severity Matrix

Severity	Safety	Environmental	Operational	Maintenance
0	No impact	No impact	No impact	No Impact
1	Near miss	Near miss	Lost production less than 1 hr.	< $1000
10	First-aid	Non-reportable incident	Lost production between 1 hr. and one half shift	Greater than $1000 but less than $10,000
100	Reportable	Internally reportable incident	Lost production greater than one half shift, less than one shift	Greater than $10,000 but less than $50,000
1000	Lost time	Externally reportable incident	Lost production greater than one shift but without substantial impact to outside customers	Greater than $50,000 but less than $100,000
10000	Death, dismemberment, or physical impairment	Major release harming environment, and involving coverage by the press	Lost production greater than one shift and impairing delivery to outside customers	Greater than $100,000

Most management teams understand what *risk* is, and they are usually risk averse. In other words, they want to make sure that any risks to the success of the business are kept to a minimum. Risk is just another word for the probability that an event will occur. In everyday maintenance speak we could say that risk is the frequency of failure of the equipment. Higher frequency of failure means we have higher risk for the consequence of the failure.

In reliability engineering terms, *criticality* is a function of the probability of failure and the severity of the consequences of the failure.

$$Criticality = f(P, S1, S2, S3 ...)$$

P = Probability of Failure   S = Severity of Consequences

In business terms, criticality is a function of risk and severity. Criticality is the best tool for helping us decide where to focus reliability resources. Therefore, criticality is the first step in determining which failures to eliminate first. This does not mean that formal criticality has to be completed prior to starting to work on failure elimination, but rather that criticality must be done early. Most organizations, if they put their minds to it, can determine where the greatest losses are occurring and start there.

Managing Failures Versus Eliminating Failures

Let's take another look at the PF curve (Figure 3-1) that describes the relationship between potential failures and functional failures.

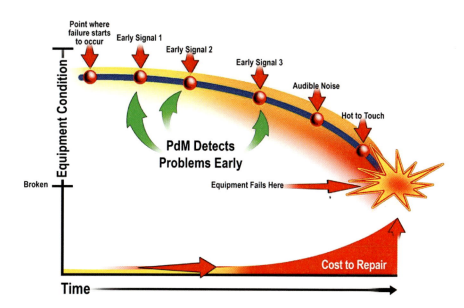

Figure 3-1: The PF Curve

Indeed, understanding this curve is an essential part of understanding how to build an effective condition-based monitoring program. Various technologies discover potential failures at different points along this curve. That knowledge helps us determine which technologies to apply where. Effective programs manage at the P end of this curve. In other words, they begin taking action as soon as the potential failure is discovered.

More reactive organizations tend to ask technicians questions like "How long before it fails? Can I make it to the end of the month so we can meet our production goal?" The problem with that line of thinking is that you are always working closer to the F, or functional failure end of the curve. This leads to more catastrophic failures and higher business risk. Looking back at the definition of failure as an unsatisfactory condition, we could say that for them, functional failures are unsatisfactory conditions, but that potential failures are not. Regardless of whether you are managing to the P or managing to the F, the fact is that failures are only being managed at this point.

> The implication for the FRACAS is that it will be harder to determine the cause of many failures because the evidence of the physical root cause is likely to be destroyed during the catastrophic failure event.

Doug Plucknette, the inventor of RCMBlitz®, developed the I-P-F curve (Figure 3-2) to reflect a change in thinking about eliminating and managing failures.

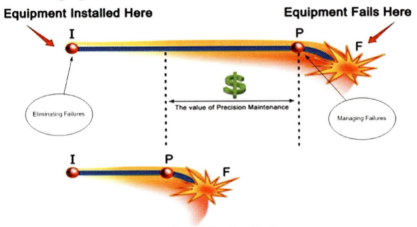

Figure 3-2: The I-P-F Curve

The I-P-F curve is important because it takes into account the impact of installing and commissioning equipment. The place to start eliminating failures is at the beginning of this curve. Now the organization will be managing to the I of the I-P-F curve. They will be eliminating instead of managing failures. How important is managing this way? The I-P-F curve holds the answer. Of the six failure curves determined by Nowlan and Heap for aircraft components (Figure 2-2) infant failures accounted for 68% of the failures. Three other studies summarized in Table 3-2 have revealed strikingly similar results.

How the U.S. Navy Began Eliminating Infant Failures

On April 10, 1963, the U.S. Navy submarine USS *Thresher* (SSN 593) was lost at sea with the loss of 129 lives. Subsequent investigation of the failure revealed that the sinking of SSN 593 may have been caused by the failure of a seawater system component that may have been improperly installed during overhaul at the shipyard. The loss of the *Thresher* resulted in the redesign of several onboard systems, and the institution of a "Submarine Safety" (SubSafe) program with detailed written procedures as its centerpiece. The Navy has not lost a single submarine due to failures in the systems covered by the SubSafe program since its inception.

Table 3-2 contains the results of Reliability studies performed on commercial aircraft, naval vessels, and manufacturing facilities. It is important to remember that the Navy started using procedures based on maintenance and operating methods on its submarines immediately after the loss of the USS *Thresher*. It is obvious that the low percentage of infant failures on their submarine fleet is most likely related to following well-written procedures and checklists.

Table 3-2: Results of Reliability vs. Age Studies
(Nowlan and Heap, Nicholas, Pau, Allen, et.al.)

Failure Curve	Aircraft		Naval Vessels		Manufacturing
	1968 UAL	1973 Broberg	1993 Surface**	2001 Submarine*	2005 Plucknette
A – Bathtub	4%	3%	3%	2%	3%
B – Wear-out	2%	1%	17%	10%	3.5%
C – Fatigue	5%	4%	3%	17%	6.5%
D – Break-in	7%	11%	6%	9%	7%
E – Random	14%	15%	42%	56%	13%
F – Infant	68%	66%	29%	6%	67%

*Data here was gathered after over 30 years of implementing the "SubSafe" Program.

**Data here was gathered approximately 15 years after the naval surface command adopted maintenance strategies similar to those used in submarines.

The Evolution of Maintenance

Maintenance of commercial aircraft and naval vessels has undergone an evolutionary change since the late 1960s. At that time maintenance strategies were heavily time based with overhauls directed at specific time-based intervals. This strategy was based on the idea that components would wear out, and if they were replaced before they reached the wear-out stage, failure could be prevented. There was growing evidence that time-based maintenance strategies were not working.

There were many instances of aircraft failures immediately after completion of overhauls. The aircraft studies done in the late 1960s and early 1970s were very compelling. What they showed was that a very low percentage of aircraft components failed in a way that was consistent with the thinking of the day. The findings in the aircraft studies revealed the startling fact that the mere act of working on the equipment could be responsible for as much as 68% of component failures.

Nowlan and Heap's work was revolutionary. Reliability-Centered Maintenance changed maintenance strategies from primarily time-based replacements and overhauls to condition-based maintenance strategies. Further, it actually made accommodations for the idea that certain components should be allowed to fail because spending resources on other types of maintenance was not cost-effective.

The Evolution of Maintenance in the U.S. Navy

Over a period of twenty years, the U.S. Navy's maintenance system evolved from a time-directed maintenance strategy relying heavily on the skill level and intuition of the people performing maintenance tasks to a condition-based procedures-driven strategy. The evolution of their strategy accounts for the differences between the early studies on commercial aircraft and the findings for naval vessels shown in Table 3-3.

Table 3-3: Evolution of Maintenance in the U.S. Navy (Nicholas)

Time Period	Event
1963	Loss of the USS *Thresher* leads to the development of the SubSafe program. The centerpiece of the program is procedure-driven maintenance that does not rely on craft knowledge and intuition.
Late 1970s	Director of Fleet Maintenance for the Naval Sea Systems Command embarks on an 18-month program to upgrade surface vessel maintenance to match the strategies used in the SubSafe program. "Controlled Work Procedures" introduced for Nuclear Submarines.
1980s	U.S. Navy adopted RCM methods converting largely time-based maintenance strategies to condition-based maintenance strategies. "Controlled Work Procedures" introduced for surface vessels.

FRACAS

In short, the U.S. Navy, by converting from time-based to condition-based maintenance, and ensuring that well-written procedures and checklists for both maintaining and operating the critical systems on their vessels, changed the distribution of failure patterns.

The State of Manufacturing

Doug Plucknette, the inventor of RCMBlitz® conducted aging studies in manufacturing during 2005 and found results very similar to those in commercial aircraft during the late 1960s and early 1970s. His findings quash the notion that aircraft and factories are "different." They do show that manufacturing is quite probably using maintenance strategies that are thirty years behind the commercial aircraft industry and the U.S. Navy. Things must change now if U.S. industry is going to survive in a global economy.

A study done in the power industry shows the pure economics of the situation. The Electric Power Research Institute (EPRI) study (Figure 3-3) revealed that maintenance costs per horsepower for a precision maintenance strategy were less than 25% of the cost of reactive maintenance, and a little over one-third the cost of a time-driven PM strategy. Precision maintenance uses a combination of RCM, Condition Monitoring, and Standards-Based Procedures to minimize maintenance costs and increase overall reliability.

Precision Maintenance – The application of skilled maintenance personnel, repeatable and effective procedures, and a failure mode driven preventive and predictive maintenance strategy to ensure equipment runs failure free for a long time.

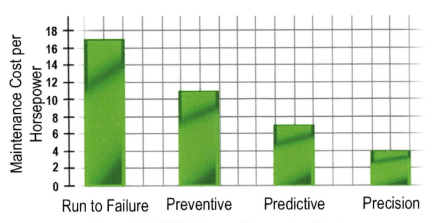

Figure 3-3: EPRI Power Generation Study

Chapter Summary

In this chapter we discussed the concept of using the consequences of failure to help determine our maintenance strategy. We saw the impact of the U.S. Navy's adoption of RCM methods to reduce the amount of maintenance required, and procedure-based maintenance and operations to reduce maintenance error. The value of adopting a precision maintenance strategy was made obvious by the EPRI study. It proves that understanding where failures come from, developing well-written procedures for dealing with those failures, and minimizing the invasiveness of maintenance tasks by using condition monitoring tools are a combination that will yield the lowest overall costs to industry.

References

Plucknette, Doug, *RCM Blitz*, Fort Myers, FL, ReliabilityWeb, 2009.

PF Curve, GPAllied, 2009.

I-P-F Curve, GPAllied, 2009.

Nicholas, Jack R., "Procedure-Based Maintenance," International Maintenance Conference, December 6, 2004.

Nowlan, F. Stanley, and Heap, Howard F., *Reliability-Centered Maintenance*, Department of Defense Report Number A066-579, December 29, 1978.

Pau, L. F., "Failure Diagnosis & Performance Monitoring," Broberg Study, Vol.11, 1981.

Allen, Tim, "U.S. Navy Analysis of Submarine Maintenance Data and the Development of Age and Reliability Profiles," nd.

Nicholas, Jack R., np, nd.

CHAPTER 4

Understanding FRACAS in Simple Terms

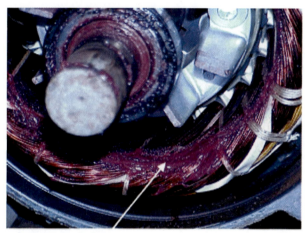
Grease on windings

Defining the Terms

Now that we have thoroughly defined what a failure is we can continue to define the FRACAS process. In order to build an effect Failure Reporting, Analysis, and Corrective Action System (FRACAS), we need to understand a couple of key words in the title.

"A failure is an unsatisfactory condition. In other words, a failure is an identifiable deviation from the original condition which is unsatisfactory to a particular user."

FRACAS must be defined so that we are capturing what our organization has defined as unacceptable conditions. Whether we choose

FRACAS

potential failures or functional failures as the unacceptable condition that we will start reporting with, has a significant bearing on how successful we will be with the failure elimination goal we establish for the FRACAS.

From Merriam-Webster we get the definitions of reporting and analysis:

> **reporting**: to make a written record or summary of
> **analysis**: an examination of a complex, its elements, and their relations

So, we are going to make written records of our failures and try to understand the elements that make up our failures so that we can understand their relationships to one another.

From the RAC *FRACAS Guide*, we get the definition of Corrective Action.

> **Corrective Action**: A [documented and validated] change in the design of a system, product, or process (including software-related designs) that is intended to reduce the rate of occurrence of failure modes.

After we find out the relationships in our failures, we are going to find some way to prevent their occurrence, document it, implement it, and validate that the change actually had the desired effect.

Last, we need to look at the definition of a system provided in the RAC's *Fault Tree Analysis Guide*:

> **System**: A composite of equipment and skills, and techniques capable of performing or supporting an operational role, or both. A complete system includes all equipment, related facilities, material, software, services, and personnel required for its operation and support to the degree that it can be considered self-sufficient in its intended operational environment.

That mouthful of a definition tells us a lot about what we need to do in order for our FRACAS to be successful. We will have to define roles, goals, and responsibilities for everyone involved with reporting, analyzing, and correcting failures. There will need to be established policies and procedures, and training to ensure that everyone knows what they are supposed to do and how they are supposed to do it. At the end of the day, the FRACAS will have to contain everything it needs to be self-sustaining in our operating environment. That is a tall order.

FRACAS is not a reporting tool or piece of software, but a process that requires all of its elements aligned in order to achieve the goal of understanding and eliminating operating system failures.

Types of Failure Reporting

Crisis Failures

In Chapter 2, we discussed the difference between chronic and crisis failures. The presence of these two types of failures means that there are two types of failure reporting as well. Crisis failures are highly visible, and can be handled by a singular type of report such as an incident report that captures the basic elements of the incident. Each incident should be ranked according to an organization's incident severity ranking index for safety, environmental, operational, and cost impact (Figure 4-1), so that they can be dealt with in a prioritized fashion

CONSEQUENCE			PROBABILITY				
People	Assets or Production	Environment	1 Improbable	2 Possible	3 Likely in next 10 years	4 Likely in next 1-2 years	5 Several times per year
First Aid/ MTC	<$10k	Slight Effect A					
Lost time accident	$10k - 100k	Minor effect B					
Perm. Disability	$100k- 500k	Localized Effect C					
Single Fatality	$500k- 10m	Major Effect D					
Multiple Fatality	>10m	Massive Effect E					

- Full Analysis required with Management Involvement
- Full Analysis with Multi-discipline team - Leader and basic composition determined by Management
- Analysis by relevant department using simple RCA tools - calling upon others where required
- Analysis by relevant department e.g. discipline, offshore operations
- No analysis required - Manage via normal Quality Procedures

Figure 4-1: Sample Incident Ranking Matrix (Hitchcock)

Crisis incidents will usually be investigated immediately to determine root causes, and corrective actions will be developed, documented, implemented, and validated.

Chronic Failures

Chronic failures are far more complex to deal with. Due to their nature, they are usually hard to ferret out, and their full business impact is usually hard to determine. The fact that many chronic failures are seen as a part of normal, everyday operations makes them even harder to deal with. A consistent failure recording system is a must for capturing and dealing with these types of failures. It is here that the importance of what constitutes an unacceptable condition to the organization pops up. Should we report on functional failures or potential failures? What is the difference? The primary difference lies in our ability to determine cause in the part-defect-cause triad.

Experience has shown that failures cost less to repair when we deal with potential failures rather than catastrophic functional failures. Quite simply, it requires less downtime, fewer resources, and fewer parts if we fix things before catastrophic failure occurs. What isn't so obvious is the difference dealing with potential failures makes in our ability to determine the parts' defects, and the causes that led to those defects. It is often very hard to determine what the defects were in parts that have been nearly demolished during the catastrophic failure, and just as hard, or nearly impossible to determine what led to the defects. It is much easier to determine defects and causes in parts that are still "whole" than it is in parts that have been severely damaged.

The point here is that setting potential failures as the unacceptable condition makes failure elimination easier in the long run, and drives the types of organizational behaviors that will nearly totally eliminate functional failures.

Understanding FRACAS in Simple Terms

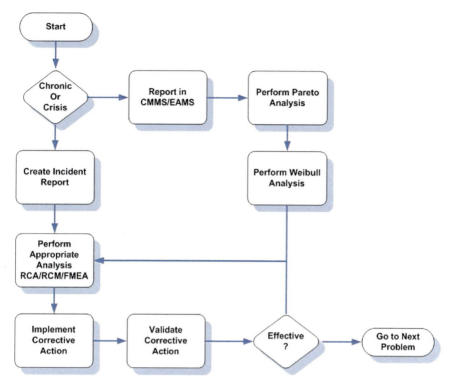

Figure 4-2: Simplified Failure Report, Analysis, and Corrective Action Flow

The important point to remember is that chronic failures require capturing and reporting capabilities so they can be found. FRACAS reports such as Mean Time Between Failures (MTBF), Mean Time to Repair (MTTR), Downtime Pareto Charts, etc., are extremely helpful in finding the problem part-defect-cause triads or failure modes. See Figure 4-2 for this process.

Types of Failure Analysis

There are two basic types of analyses that can be done on failures. There is *statistical analysis* which will help us determine the type and extent of the problems, and *failure elimination analysis* which will help us reduce the level of failures in the organization.

FRACAS

Statistical Analysis Methods

1. Pareto Analysis (Figure 4-3: Pareto Example)

One of the most useful forms of statistical analysis we can use is Pareto Analysis. It is the single type of analysis that can help sort out the causes of our greatest losses so that we can focus on solving those problems that have the greatest return on the investment of time, money, and people that is required to solve complex problems. Care should be taken to ensure that the correct attributes are charted. Numbers of work orders and MTBF don't give a complete picture. There has to be some provision for analyzing total downtime or total overall costs, including lost production. Remember, everything is interrelated, and we have to focus on **the business impact** of the failures. It is also important to look for commonality or common threads across the organization. Do you have a lot of bearing defects related to inadequate lubrication?

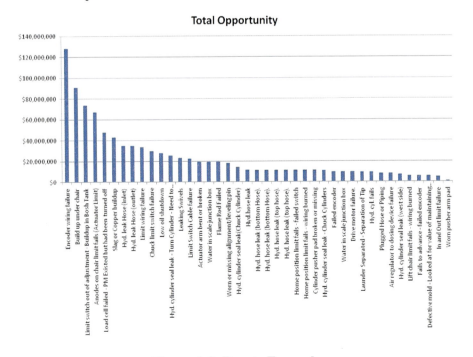

Figure 4-3: Pareto Example

2. Weibull Analysis
(Figure 4-4: Sample Weibull Failure Rate Plot)

Another useful statistical tool is Weibull Analysis. It is probably one of the most misunderstood tools around. It has only become well-known in everyday industry during the past five years or so. It is actually very simple to use, especially if we employ software tools to do it. If we are collecting good failure modes data, we can determine what types of failures are dominant in the facility, and can make adjustments based on that knowledge. As we saw in previous chapters there seems to be a dominance of infant failures across many industries due to the lack of precision maintenance techniques. The data can tell us whether we need to do RCA to determine root causes of our dominant failures, whether we have an across-the-board systemic issue, or whether we have issues related to even a specific brand and type of equipment.

The true beauty of Weibull lies in the fact that it requires very few data points. That is an important characteristic for those of us in the failure prevention business since a data point equals a failure.

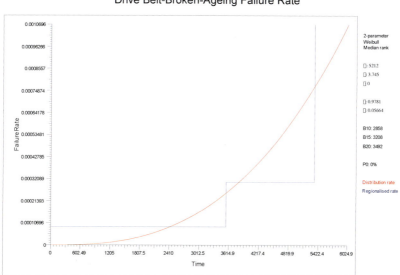

Figure 4-4: Sample Weibull Failure Rate Plot

FRACAS

Failure Elimination Analysis

Once the predominant failures have been determined, they have to be eliminated. The primary method used for this is Root Cause Analysis (RCA). It is possible that an entire system may be having multiple issues. A case like this might lead us to use Reliability Centered Maintenance (RCM), or Failure Modes and Effects Analysis (FMEA) to develop a new maintenance strategy for the entire system.

Root Cause Analysis

There are multiple methods for performing RCA. Each method has advantages, and drawbacks that need to be dealt with in order to achieve a successful analysis and solution.

> *"It is not root causes we seek, it is effective solutions"*
> - Leith Hitchcock

Table 4-1 provides a useful guideline for selecting an appropriate method of RCA depending on the size and type of problem you are trying to solve.

Understanding FRACAS in Simple Terms

Table 4-1: RCA Tehnique Selection (Hitchcock)	
Situation	**Techniques**
Simple problems Relatively obvious sequence of events with ample evidence	5 Whys Difference Analysis
Obscure cause Organizational behavior breakdown	Change Analysis Difference Analysis (useful in all analyses)
Complex barriers and controls Procedural or administrative problems	Barrier Analysis MORT Logic Tree
Multifaceted problems with long causal factor chains	Causal Tree Analysis Fault Tree Analysis
People problems	Human Performance Evaluation MORT Logic Tree Fishbone Diagram
Thorough analysis of both causes and corrective actions	Kepner-Tregoe

Corrective Action Selection

Our goal for any failure analysis is to find a solution that will either eliminate the failure, or get the failure rate down to a level that is acceptable to the organization. Every problem may have several possible solutions, and some problems may require multiple corrective actions to get the desired result. It is important to remember that every corrective action must be tested for applicability and effectiveness. We can start this process by looking at the RCM task guidelines originally established in the Nowlan and Heap work cited earlier.

39

FRACAS

Table 4-2: Applicability and Effectiveness Criteria (Nowlan and Heap)

Characteristic	On-Condition Task	Scheduled Rework Task	Scheduled Discard Task	Failure-Finding Task
Applicability Criteria	Reduced resistance to failure must be detectable; rate of reduction in failure resistance must be predictable.	Conditional probability of failure must increase at an identifiable age; a large proportion of the units must survive to that age.	For safe-life items, conditional probability of failure must be zero below life limit; for economic-life items conditional probability of failure must increase at an identifiable age and a large proportion of units must survive to that age.	The occurrence of a functional failure must not be evident to the operating crew.
Effectiveness Criteria	For critical failures, the task must reduce the risk of failure to an acceptable level; in all other cases the task must be cost-effective.	For critical failures the task must reduce the risk of failure to an acceptable level (a rework task alone is unlikely to meet this requirement); in all other cases the task must be cost-effective.	A safe-life limit must reduce the risk of failure to an acceptable level; an economic-life limit must be cost-effective.	The task must result in the level of availability necessary to reduce the risk of a multiple failure to an acceptable level.

Certainly these criteria would apply to any changes made to the basic maintenance strategy for the failure mode being analyzed, but the basic philosophy of applicability and effectiveness can be applied to any corrective action. In short, to be applicable, the corrective action must have some basis in fact related to what caused the failure in the first place, and to be effective it must prevent the failure from occurring again or reduce failures to an acceptable level. For safety (environmental) related failures it must reduce recurrence to zero. For failures with economic consequences only, it must be cost-effective.

There may be several alternative solutions to choose from for corrective actions. Selection criteria should be established ahead of time based on the characteristics of the minimum acceptable solution characteristics and the desired solution characteristics. This is best done by creating a characteristics list that consists of musts and wants. Any solution that does not meet the musts can be immediately eliminated. Other solutions can be rank-ordered based on where they score on the desired characteristics list after having met the musts.

Table 4-3: Sample Solution Selection Matrix (Hitchcock & Kepner-Tregoe)

Solution Criteria		Alternatives							
MUSTS		Alt A		Alt B		Alt C		Alt D	
Must Achieve									
Must Maintain									
Must Avoid									
WANTS	Weight Factor	Raw score	Wgt. score	Raw score	Wgt. score	Raw score	Wgt. score	Raw score	Wgt. score
Want to Achieve									
Want to Maintain									
Want to Avoid									
Total Weighted Score									

Chapter Summary

In this chapter we used the definitions of the individual words in the FRACAS title to gain an understanding of what a FRACAS really is. The important takeaway from that discussion is that the FRACAS must be well defined with roles, goals, and responsibilities for all involved. At some point, the organization has to define whether corrective actions are developed for functional failures only, or for potential failures as well. Any organization that wants to achieve zero functional failures must develop corrective actions that will eliminate potential failures.

FRACAS

We also discussed the two basic types of analyses that occur. Statistical analysis is used to understand the business impact of the failures so decisions can be made about which ones should have failure elimination analysis applied to them. Corrective actions will generally consist of either changes to the system design, changes to maintenance strategies, or changes to operating procedures. It is very important to ensure that any changes meet the organization's applicability and effectiveness criteria.

References

DOE Guideline DOE-NE-STD-1004-92, <u>Root Cause Analysis Guidance Document,</u> February 1992.

Kepner, C.H., and Tregoe, B., *The New Rational Manager*, Princeton, NJ: Princeton Research Press, 1981.

Hitchcock, Leith, "GPAllied RCA Methods Guide," 2009.

Nowlan, F. Stanley, and Heap, Howard F., *Reliability-Centered Maintenance*, Department of Defense Report Number A066-579, December 29, 1978.

CHAPTER 5

Failure Reports

With anything we want to develop, we must start with the end in mind. Using failure reporting, the analysis of failure data is used to take corrective action which is required to eliminate or mitigate a failure by executing Root Cause Analysis (RCA), or the development of a new Equipment Maintenance Plan (EMP) as a result of the findings (see Figure 5-1, FRACAS Process).

FRACAS

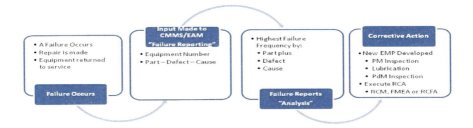

Figure 5-1: The FRACAS Process.

The objective of FRACAS is to identify, eliminate, and/or mitigate failures which prevent an organization from meeting its financial, environmental, and safety performance goals through a formalized process.

Failure Reporting

Failure reports are used in the analysis and corrective action phase of FRACAS. Failure reporting can come in many forms. The key is to have a disciplined plan to review failure reports in a specific time period and develop action to eliminate failure.

Failure Report Examples (all included as part of your FRACAS Continuous Improvement and Defect Elimination Process):

1. **Asset Health** or **Percent of Assets with No Identifiable Defects** reported by maintenance management to plant and production management on a monthly basis at least. An asset that has an identifiable defect is said to be in a condition RED. An asset that does not have an identifiable defect is said to be in condition GREEN. That is it. It is that simple. There are no other "but ifs," "what ifs," or "if /thens." If there is an identifiable defect, the asset is in condition RED. If there is no identifiable defect, it is GREEN. The percentage of machines that are in condition GREEN is the asset health (as a percentage) for that plant or area. See the example in Figure 5-2

Defect: an abnormality in a part which leads to equipment or asset failure if not corrected in time

44

Asset Health Summary
From: Jun 2006 To: Jun 2007
View: Overall

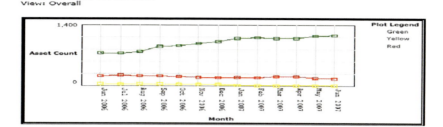

Figure 5-2: Percent of Assets with No Identifiable Defect

Example: The plant has 1,000 pieces of equipment. Of that number, 750 of them have no identifiable defects. The plant is said to have 75% asset health. There is an interesting aspect about asset health. Once this change is underway, asset health, as a metric becomes what most maintenance managers and plant managers have wanted for a long time—a leading indicator of maintenance costs and business risk.

2. **Mean Time Between Failures, Mean Time To Repairs, and Mean Time Between Repairs** reported by maintenance or reliability engineers on a monthly basis on the top 5% to 20 % of critical equipment. By combining these three metrics you can identify if you may have a problem with equipment repairs. If the equipment repairs on repetitive failures have a low Mean Time Between Failure (MTBF), then something is wrong with the repair process or failure modes strategy. It could be time to repair (MTTR) procedure, specifications, or standards, or something else if the true cause of these failures is based on variation. Mean Time Between Repairs (MTBR) can be used to calculate maintenance equipment availability.

FRACAS

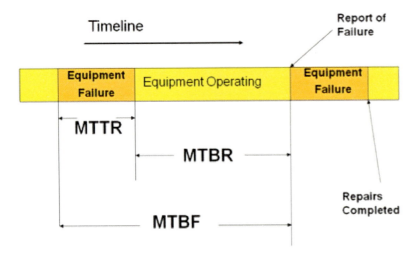

Figure 5-3

3. **Mean Time Between Failure By Plant, Area, System, and Equipment Type**

   (MTBF) can provide valuable feedback to leadership and craft personnel telling them if maintenance and reliability efforts are having an effect on equipment reliability. If MTBF is rising because of a new initiative this could be a positive sign. If MTBF is reducing then you have a negative response. MTBF is a good indication that your PM program is working in an area if your "bad actor" program is having any effect on the reliability of your equipment. Typically, MTBF is the first indication things are getting better or worse because small breakdowns (which may be hidden) can lead to large breakdowns. (See "MTBF Users Guide" under "Help Documents" at the end of the book.)

4. **Cost Variance by Area of the Plant** reported by the maintenance and production supervisor's area of responsibility. *Cost variance must be reported to maintenance and production management on a monthly basis.* The report should not be acceptable without a known cause of the variance and a plan to bring it into compliance.

Mechanical Maintenance Budget Variance Report

Area	Actual	Budgeted	Variance
Overhead Cranes	123,454	110,000	(13,454)
Cast House	333,786	432,008	98,222
Crushers	192,000	139,975	(52,025)
Mobile Equipment	56,000	87,800	31,800

Figure 5-4

5. **Most Frequent Part-Defect-Cause Report** is reported monthly by maintenance or reliability engineers. If you do not have maintenance or reliability engineers, you may need to appoint a couple of your best maintenance technicians as reliability engineering technicians, even if unofficially, and train them to be a key player in this failure elimination process. This one report can identify *common failure threads* or *failure patterns* within your operation and when resolved can make a quick impact on failure elimination and can increase reliability.

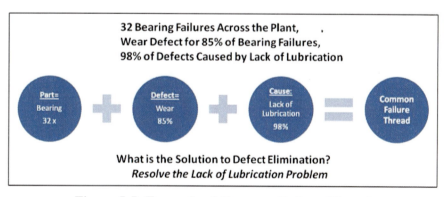

Figure 5-5: Example of Common Failure Thread by Part-Defect-Cause

6. **Most Dominant Failure Pattern Identification:** In 1978, United Airlines, under sponsorship with the U.S. Department of Defense, released a study on reliability defining six failure patterns, with infant mortality being the highest. These failure patterns are shown in Figure 5-6. Knowing the dominant failure pattern in an

organization is key to knowing where to focus your efforts to reduce, eliminate, or mitigate failures. This process is simply accomplished by using Weibull Analysis.

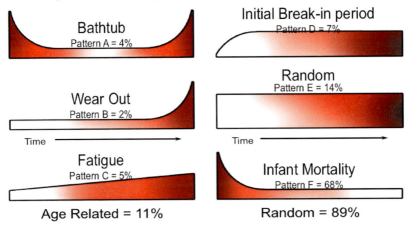

Figure 5-6

Once you know your most dominant failure pattern, then you develop a Pareto chart of the components with similar causes of failures which created this pattern. Now you can make a huge impact on the reliability of your equipment.

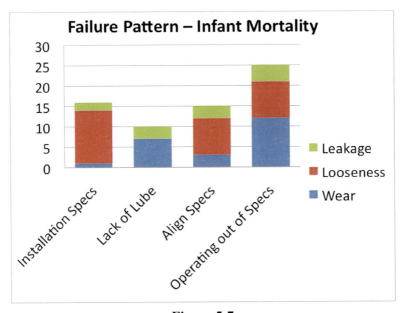

Figure 5-7

In the example for infant mortality, one would find in this Pareto where operating out of specifications is causing the greatest failure. The solution may be to retrain operators on the operating criteria for this pump along with providing them with the Pareto charts for failures.

Chapter Summary

Failure reports must be identified before your work can begin. Make sure what you measure has a process by which everyone knows who is accountable, responsible, consulted, and informed. Never think a software tool will solve your problems. It is only by disciplined leadership that Failure Reporting, Analysis, and Corrective Action Systems can become effective.

Weibull Analysis
(Everything you wanted to know but were afraid to ask)

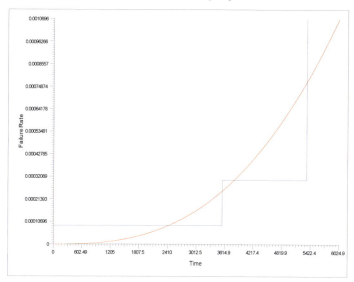

Figure 6-1

Introduction to Weibull Analysis

The Weibull distribution is a widely recognized statistical distribution created by Swedish born Waloddi Weibull to describe life distributions. The primary advantage of the distribution is that it requires very small amounts of data when compared with other forms of statistical analysis. It could be said that the primary job of physical asset man-

FRACAS

agers is to prevent failures. Stated another way, the primary job of physical asset managers is to prevent data points for failure analysis. A statistical method that is effective using small amounts of data is a very useful tool for understanding equipment failures.

Equipment fails based on its basic design, and on how it reacts to the way it is operated and maintained. This relationship means there is a direct relationship between maintenance and operating activities and the Weibull shapes that are present in plant equipment. This chapter will discuss basic Weibull shapes, how operating and maintenance activities impact them, and the steps organizations can take to change those shapes to meet the needs of the business for equipment availability.

The Bathtub Curve

The Bathtub Curve consists of three distinct regions. Each region contains its own unique values for the Weibull parameters; Eta, Beta, and Gamma. The Weibull parameters provide insight into the failure mechanism that is present.

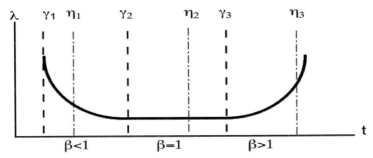

Figure 6-2: The Bathtub Curve with Weibull Parameters

Table 6-1: Weibull Parameter Definitions

Weibull Parameter	Description
Gamma (γ) or Location Parameter	Gives the location of each section of the Weibull curve. Gamma 3 is particularly important for items with a wear-out mechanism because it marks the beginning of the zone of increasing failure rate.
Beta (β) or Shape Factor	Beta values are an indicator of the failure behavior of the component. Beta values less than one represent infant failures, Beta values equal to one represent random failures, and Beta values greater than one represent wear-out failures.
Eta (η) or Characteristic Life	Eta gives an estimate of how long components might last after being put into service. It represents the point in time where 63.2% of the components in service are likely to have failed.

What do Beta values tell us?

Beta values are extremely important because they tell us the failure behavior of the component. Knowledge of the failure behavior will lead us down a certain path when trying to improve overall reliability and availability.

Infant Failures

Beta less than one, or infant failure, indicates that there may be a quality issue present among our maintenance, operating, or spare parts acquisition programs. There is no time-based maintenance activity we can do for these types of failures until we determine the root cause or causes of the infant failures. Our goal is to eliminate or minimize the high early failure rate represented by the curve.

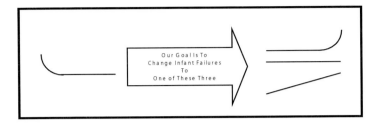

Figure 6-3: Changing Infant Failures to Random or Wear-out

There is a large laundry list of possible causes of infant failure mechanisms. Table 2 gives some examples of the potential sources of infant failures.

Table 6-2: Potential Organizational Causes for Infant Failures	
Source	**Causes**
Maintenance Activities	• No, or inadequate, quality of work control procedures and policies • Unskilled or untrained maintainers • No, or poorly written, maintenance procedures • Poor organizational communication • No focus on precision maintenance • Inadequate maintenance supervision
Operating Activities	• No, or inadequate, operating procedures, especially start-up procedures • Unskilled or untrained operators • Inadequate operations supervision
Procurement Activities	• Procurement focused solely on price • No, or inadequate, quality control procedures for incoming spares, especially custom manufactured parts from third-party vendors • Parts procured from a wide variety of vendors

High Failure Rate Random Failures

Random failures are characterized by a Beta value of approximately one. High failure rate random failures have a shorter than expected, or shorter than desired characteristic life, or Eta. Random failures typically lend themselves to either route-based, or constant-condition monitoring, but still may have a greater than desired negative impact on the goals of the organization if the failure rate is too high.

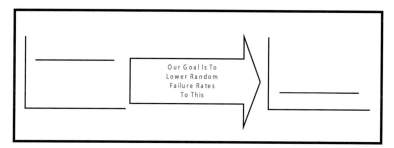

Figure 6-4: Reducing Random Failure Rates

Random failures are usually caused by some outside action that induces failures into the component. The organizational activities listed in Table 6-3 are some likely sources of higher than expected or desired random failure rates.

FRACAS

Table 6-3: Potential Organizational Causes for High Random Failure Rates

Source	Causes
Maintenance Activities	• Lubrication routes not well designed • Inconsistent torque applied to bolts • Poor maintenance cleanliness practices • Inadequate lightning protection
Operating Activities	• Equipment occasionally operated outside its design envelope • Process upsets created by inadequate quality control of incoming raw materials • Process upsets created by unskilled or untrained operators
Procurement Activities	• Parts procured from a wide variety of vendors • Parts specifications not clear

Short Life Wear-out Failures (Early Wear-out)

Generally, wear-out failures lend themselves to some sort of time-based replacement or overhaul strategy. Wear-out, even though it is predictable, can have a significant negative impact on the goals of the organization if components are not lasting as long as they are expected or desired to.

Figure 6-5: Extending the Wear-out Curve

Early wear-out is often caused by a lack of understanding of the stresses present in the equipment during the design phase, but there are organizational activities that can lead to early component wear-out.

Table 6-4: Potential Organizatioal Causes for Early Wear-out

Source	Causes

Maintenance Activities	• Under-lubrication of bearings
	• Using incorrect lubricant for the service
	• Over-lubrication of bearings
	• Service intervals too long for:
	    Lubrication
	    Adjustments
	• Consistent over- tightening of belts
	• Consistent over-torquing of bolts
	• Using parts below required specifications

Operating Activities	• Consistently operating the equipment outside its design envelope
Procurement Activities	• Purchasing spares below needed specifications

How Do I Know What I Have?

(How to build Weibull shapes with no data)

Many companies do not have the necessary data to complete Weibull analysis on their failing components. They do have experienced personnel in maintenance and operations who are knowledgeable about what fails, and how it fails. The trick to building the Weibull shapes without data is to learn what questions to ask the maintainers and operators.

FRACAS

Table 6-5: Some Simple Questions for Determining Weibull Failure Mechanisms

Question	Answer	What the Answer Tells Us
1. How many times have you repaired this particular failure in the last three years?	A number	The answer gives an approximation of the Mean-Time Between Failures or the characteristic life. It may not be exact, but it will be close enough for making a reasonable decision.
2. If you work on it today, do you know you have to warn others that you worked on it because it may not get through till the day after tomorrow?	Yes	There is probably an infant failure mechanism present. You will need to do some (RCA) to determine why and eliminate the cause.
3. If you work on it today, do you know you won't have to come back to work on it again until sometime near the Mean Time To Failure you determined in question one? If you wait too long after that will it probably fail?	Yes	This is probably a wear-out failure. It can most likely be addressed with a time-based replacement or overhaul strategy, but RCA should be performed to find root cause if the wear-out is occurring sooner than desired.
4. If you work on it today, is it likely to fail sometime between now and the Mean Time To Failure determined in question one, but you can't be certain that it will last that long?	Yes	This is most likely a random failure. It can be handled by condition monitoring unless the failure rate is higher than is tolerable for the organization. If the rate is too high, then RCFA should be performed to find and eliminate the cause.

Changing the Failure Mechanisms

Changing failure mechanisms requires effort on multiple levels. At the outset, the immediate causes of the failures must be addressed so that repetition of the failure does not occur. Eventually the organizational or latent causes need to be removed in order to ensure that the conditions originally allowing the failure mechanisms to be present are removed.

Table 6-6: Actions You Can Take to Change Your Weibull Shapes

Action	Benefit	Cautions
Root Cause Failure Analysis (RCFA) or Causal Analysis	• Will uncover the physical, human, and latent roots of the failures. • Will help lower or remove the infant failures so that an effective maintenance tactic can be developed.	RCFA must be viewed and managed as a program, not as a thing to do. There must be well-defined policies and procedures that are followed to ensure that the right things are analyzed, and that recommendations furthering the organization's goals are implemented in a timely fashion.
Establish a Maintenance Quality Control Program	• Will help ensure that maintainers are focused on quality and workmanship, and that controls are in place to help ensure the quality of completed work. • Will help eliminate repeat work. • Will help lower or remove the infant failures so that an effective maintenance tactic can be developed.	The QC program has to establish guidelines for what constitutes good quality, and contain sufficient auditing to ensure that the program is carried out. First line supervision must be made aware of the importance of their role in ensuring the quality of maintenance work. The QC program should be developed by a team consisting of craft, supervision, and management to help get maximum buy-in for the program.

continued....

FRACAS

continued from page 59....

Table 6-6: Actions You Can Take to Change Your Weibull Shapes

Action	Benefit	Cautions
Establish a Training Program for Maintainers and Operators	• Will help ensure that the maintainers and operators understand the best operating and maintaining practices, and that they understand the impact of their behaviors on equipment failures. • Will help lower or remove the infant failures so that an effective maintenance tactic can be developed. • Will help lower the failure rate for some random failures.	Great care must be taken to ensure that the program addresses the competencies required, and the level of skill required in each competency. The use of competency maps is highly recommended to ensure that the right people get the right level of training for the least amount of resources expended. There may be some immediate training that will eliminate a particular failure, but the overall program will require vision and a focus on future results.
Establish Written Procedures for Maintaining Equipment	• Will help insure that maintenance jobs have repeatability and that there is some consistency in job quality. • Will help lower or remove the infant failures so that an effective maintenance tactic can be developed.	The written procedures must contain enough information to complete jobs properly without insulting the intelligence of the craftspeople. Procedures are best developed by a team consisting of craftspeople, planners, and procurement specialists. There must be an established audit process to ensure that the procedures are kept up to date.

continued....

continued from page 60....

Table 6-6: Actions You Can Take to Change Your Weibull Shapes

Action	Benefit	Cautions
Establish Written Procedures for Operating Equipment	• Will help ensure that equipment is operated within a set range of parameters, and that equipment shutdown and startup is accomplished in a way that minimizes negative impact on equipment reliability • Will help lower or remove the infant failures so that an effective maintenance tactic can be developed	The written procedures must ensure that both new and seasoned operators have enough information available to operate the equipment as desired. They are best developed by a team consisting of maintainers and operators so that the implications of operating the equipment in a certain way are well understood.
Establish a Quality Control Program for Spares Procurement	• Will help ensure that procured spares meet at least the minimum specifications required to establish the desired level of equipment reliability • Will help lower or remove the infant failures so that an effective maintenance tactic can be developed	The spares QC program is best developed by a team consisting of maintainers and procurement specialists. It is important to make sure that those responsible for procuring parts understand the full implications of their purchasing decisions. There must be established quality criteria for parts manufactured by third-party vendors, especially machined parts. It is important to perform quality inspections on the incoming parts to ensure that they meet engineering specifications.

continued....

FRACAS

continued from page 61....

Table 6-6: Actions You Can Take to Change Your Weibull Shapes

Action	Benefit	Cautions
Establish a Lubricant Management Program	• Will help ensure that the correct lubricant is applied in the correct amount at the correct point at the correct interval, and that it is clean. • Will help lower the failure rate for some random failure. • Will provide life extension for some early wear-out failures.	Establishing a lubricant management program is not a simple task. It is not enough to simply establish lubrication routes. In most cases extensive training is required to ensure good results.

Chapter Summary

The questioning method for building Weibull shapes gives you a good starting point in the absence of hard data, but it is not a perfect replacement for hard data. Hard data along with analysis of the impact or effects of the failures will allow you to sharpen maintenance tactics and strategies to move you closer to achieving your business goals.

The key things to remember are that the failure mechanisms present in your equipment are a reflection of the maintenance, operating, and procurement activities present within your organization, and that there is a direct link between best maintenance and operating practices, and changing the Weibull behavior of your equipment.

CHAPTER 7

Steps to Implementing an Effective FRACAS

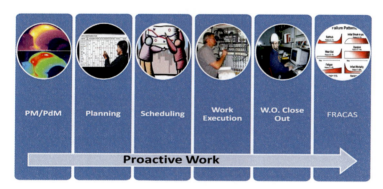

Figure 7-1: Proactive Work

FRACAS Checklist

The foundational elements of an effective FRACAS are:

- ☐ Equipment hierarchy built and validated so that similar failures on like equipment can be identified across an organization.
- ☐ Criticality analysis developed and validated so that equipment criticality is ranked based on production throughput, asset utilization, cost, environment, and safety.
- ☐ Failure modes analysis completed on all critical equipment using FMA, FMEA, or RCM.
- ☐ Equipment maintenance plans developed on all critical equipment to prevent or predict a failure.

FRACAS

- ☐ Failure codes followed to ensure failure elimination efforts are focused on correct causes of failures.
- ☐ Effective Planning and Scheduling applied and followed in a disciplined approach.
- ☐ RACI chart developed to ensure everyone knows who is accountable, who is responsible, who is consulted, and who is informed.
- ☐ Failure reports identified for the organization.
- ☐ Accurate data input into the CMMS/EAM for the reports needed.

Five Steps to Building a Failure Elimination/Mitigation Program

STEP 1: Effective Equipment Hierarchy

Asset catalog or equipment hierarchy must be developed to provide the data required to manage a proactive maintenance program. The equipment hierarchy should be developed based on site, areas, systems, assets, and component. A manager should be able to see from a high level any part of his/her process which is beginning to show a problem through Mean Time Between Failure and Cost. They need the ability to drive down to the lowest level to understand where the problem is located in order to ask valid questions to their subordinates.

NOTE: In addition, you need know the parts required by number. For example: a 50HP motor with a specific frame size, voltage, etc. is needed for a motor failure. It is found that a similar motor is found in the warehouse, however the part number is different in the CMMS/EAM. After 70-90 days, the motor fails again and the process begins again to locate another motor. The problem was that no one specified the type of bearing required for the motor. If a cylindrical roller bearing is used in a motor then it is used for a belt drive application. If a deep-groove roller bearing is used, then it is used for a direct coupled drive. Using either of these bearings (same motor size, etc.) will cause premature failure. Instead of the motor lasting 8-10 years it will only last 70-90 days. Equipment hierarchy requires all the nameplate and vendor data in order to eliminate failures.

In order to eliminate failures, one needs to ensure this is a successful first step. Figure 7-2 shows how FRACAS can be used to resolve specific causes of plantwide failures by the identification of the part, failure code, and cause. In this illustration, we see a "Part – Bearing" from different size electric motors with 27 total failures ("Part" as identified on CMMS/EAM Codes drop-down menus). One type "Defect – Wear" occurred in 18 out of 27 failures ("Defect" or Failure Mode, as identified on CMMS/EAM Codes drop-down menus). "Cause – Lack of Lubrication" was found to be the cause of all 18 of those failures ("Cause" as identified on CMMS/EAM Codes drop-down menus). If we solve the "Lack of Lubrication" problem, we can solve issues with bearings across the site quickly.

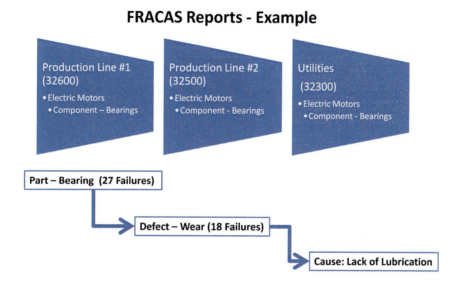

Figure 7-2: **Reason for Equipment Hierarchy Validated**

"After a thorough analysis one will find that most failures come from a small amount of equipment. The question is: 'Which equipment?'"
– Andy Page, CMRP

STEP 2: Asset Criticality Analysis

Everyone says they have identified their critical equipment. Equipment criticality, in many cases, could change based on how upset people are about an equipment problem, or if people are confused about what consequences are associated with a failure and the probability it will occur if we manage equipment reliability effectively.

FRACAS

The purpose of Asset Criticality Analysis is to identify what equipment has the most serious potential consequences on business performance if it fails and has had the most failures. Consequences on the business include:

- Production throughput or equipment/facility utilization
- Cost due to lost or reduced output
- Environmental issues
- Safety issues
- Other

The resulting equipment criticality number is used to prioritize resources performing maintenance work. The Intercept Ranking Model illustrates this process (Figure 7-3). On the "Y" axis you see the asset criticality is listed from none to high. It uses a scale of 0-1000 because all assets are not necessarily equal.

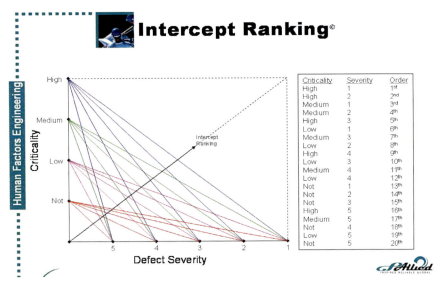

Figure 7-3: Intercept Model

The only other two factors I would add in determining which job to plan or schedule would be based on work order type (PM, CM, CBM, Rebuild, etc.) plus time on back. Figure 7-4 shows the 4-Way Prioritization Model for planning and scheduling

Identify which equipment is most likely to negatively impact business performance because it matters a lot when it fails, and it fails frequently. The resulting relative risk number is used to identify candidate assets for reliability improvement.

4-Way Prioritization Model

Asset Criticality	Defect Severity	Time on Backlog	Work Order Type
500 – Highest Criticality	5 – Priority 1 (Most Severe)	4 – Greater than 120 Days	10 - Emergency
	4 – Priority 2	3 – Greater than 90 Days	9 – Quality Compliance
1 – Lowest Criticality	3 – Priority 3	2 – Greater than 60 Days	8 – Results of PdM Inspection
	4 – Priority 4	1 – Less than 60 Days	7 – Preventive Maintenance Inspections
	1 – Priority 5 (Least Severe)		6 – Working Conditions/Safety
			5 – Planned Work Outage
			4 – Normal Maintenance
			3 – Projects and Experiments
			2 – Cost Reductions
			1 – Spares Equipment

Figure 7-4: 4-Way Prioritization Model

A consistent definition for equipment criticality needs to be adopted and validated in order to ensure the right work is completed at the right time. This is key to the elimination of failures. The definition of critical equipment may vary from organization to organization. In fact, if it is not formalized there may be several interpretations of equipment criticality within a single organization. The assumptions used to assess what equipment is critical are not technically based. As a result, when different individuals are asked to identify their critical equipment, they will likely select different pieces of equipment. Often we are told, "All of our equipment is critical!" Selections are based on individual opinions, lacking consensus. The potential for equipment failure having significant safety, environmental, or economic consequences may be overlooked.

A consistent definition for equipment criticality needs to be adopted. The definition used in the context of this document is:

"Critical equipment is that equipment whose failure has the highest potential impact on the business goals of the company."
– Ron Thomas, Dofasco Steel

FRACAS

The relationship between equipment failure and business performance is an important factor in deciding where and when resources should be applied to maintain or improve equipment reliability.

Maintaining reliable equipment performance requires the timely execution of maintenance work to proactively address the causes of equipment failure. Large organizations normally manage a backlog of maintenance work. This maintenance work is made up of individual tasks that must be carried out over limited time periods, using limited resources. The maintenance scheduling function strives to optimize the application of resources to get all the "right work done at the right time." Effective maintenance scheduling requires an understanding of how critical the equipment is that the task is applied to, so that a priority can be assigned to each job. The criticality is a function of the potential consequence that could occur if the job is not completed within the required time frame.

Equipment reliability improvement also requires the application of either human or financial resources. The business case for improvement justifies why the limited resources of the company should be applied to a project over the many possible alternatives that exist that are also competing for usually the same resources. When justifying an improvement project, it is not sufficient to demonstrate benefit. It is necessary to demonstrate that the relative benefits of a project exceed the potential benefits of other projects.

Equipment reliability improvement projects benefit the organization by reducing the consequences of failure and/or reducing the probability that the failure will occur. Equipment reliability improvement projects must focus on equipment that both matters a lot when it fails and is failing a lot. The combination of failure consequence and failure probability is a measure of the risk posed to the organization by the specified equipment.

Why use the concept of "risk" to prioritize equipment reliability improvement projects? Alternate approaches used to identify which equipment could benefit from some form of reliability improvement usually use only failure frequency data or failure consequence data (FRACAS). Equipment failures are analyzed to identify which equipment has the greatest number of failures or to identify which equipment is causing the most "pain." The most frequent measure of "pain" is economic impact. Focus is directed on the equipment which is costing us the most money. "Pain" can also be related to other consequences such as the number of safety or environmental incidents. The problem with this approach is that focus is restricted to historical events.

The discipline of Risk Management recognizes that failures with high consequence normally occur infrequently, while failures with low consequence occur more frequently. The consequence of a failure is plotted against the probability of the failure event. Probability is a measure of the number of events/unit time. The probability of an event like the nuclear submarine *Thresher* accident is very low but the consequence is very high. Consequently, we don't see a high frequency of accidents with this severity.

STEP 3: Identification of Failure Modes

The goal of most maintenance strategies is to prevent or predict equipment failures. The primary goal of an effective Preventive (PM) or Predictive Maintenance (PdM) Program is to prevent or predict specific failure modes, or for regulatory compliance. Most companies have PM programs, however, most of them do not address specific failure modes.

For example: an electric motor with roller bearings has specific failure modes which can be prevented with lubrication. The failure mode is "wear" caused by "lack of lubrication." The next question may be why you had lack of lubrication. The lack of lubrication could be identified as a result of no lubrication standard being established for bearings. In other words someone gives the bearing "x" amount of shots of grease even though no one knows the exact amount to prevent the bearing from failure.

The best way to identify failure modes when developing a maintenance strategy is to apply Reliability Centered Maintenance (RCM) or Failure Modes and Effect Analysis (FMEA). Typically 10%–20% of assets are critical and should have RCM applied to them. FMEA can be applied to the other 80%–90%. The difference between FMEA and RCM is FMEA looks at "how the equipment fails and the effect it has on the system." RCM applies the same strategy as FMEA, however it includes the operating context and operating environment.

The problem most companies identify is that most of their new maintenance strategies are preventive maintenance in nature when they should have applied predictive maintenance. You will find most maintenance strategies are not focused on prevention and prediction of failure modes.

Another problem is that most companies do not have the data to identify a major problem on multiple assets. (No data in equals no effective failure reports out.) It isn't the motor that failed; it failed because of a specific part's failure mode which resulted in catastrophic damage to the motor unless the defect was identified early enough in the failure mode.

STEP 4: Develop a Maintenance Strategy

The maintenance strategy is a result of a Failure Modes and Effect Analysis (FMEA), Reliability Centered Maintenance (RCM), or as a result of failure data from your CMMS/EAM.

> **Elimination Strategy:** The best way to eradicate failures is to get a better understanding of the true nature of the equipment's failure patterns and adjust the *maintenance strategy* to match.
> –Andy Page, CMRP

So what is a maintenance strategy? Let's break down the two words:

Maintenance is to maintain or keep in an existing condition; to keep, preserve, protect.

Strategy is development of a prescriptive plan toward a specific goal.

A maintenance strategy is a prescriptive plan to protect equipment from failure by identifying the best solution for specific equipment which results in optimized reliability at optimal cost. Less invasive is preferred to more invasive. This is one of the fundamental concepts of any well-defined maintenance strategy. Specific maintenance strategies are designed to mitigate the consequences of each failure mode. As a result, maintenance is viewed as a reliability function instead of a repair function. Saying this means Predictive Maintenance or Condition Monitoring is the best solution because it is mainly noninvasive.

Knowing that both systemic problems and operating envelope problems produce the same type of defects, a maintenance strategy that merely attempts to discover the defects and correct them will never be able to reach a proactive state. Technicians will be too busy fixing the symptoms of problems instead of addressing the root cause. To reach a truly proactive state, the root cause of the defects will need to be identified and eliminated. Maintenance strategies that accomplish this are able to see the step change in performance and achieve incredible cost savings. Maintenance strategies that do not attempt to address the root cause of defects will continue to see lackluster results and struggle with financial performance.

A maintenance strategy involves everyone utilizing a prescriptive plan in order to meet a common goal. Key parts of a maintenance strategy include:

- Preventive and predictive maintenance based on a solid failure mode elimination strategy.
- Maintenance planning which includes repeatable procedures.
- Work scheduling based on equipment criticality and defect severity.
- Execution of work using precision techniques to include proper commissioning of equipment when a new part or equipment is installed to ensure no defect is identified after this event occurs.

The very last part of your maintenance strategy is FRACAS (Failure Reporting, Analysis, and Corrective Action System) because it involves the continuous improvement portion of this strategy.

Preventive and Predictive Maintenance

Preventive Maintenance or Predictive Maintenance (or Condition Monitoring) is the maintenance strategy used to prevent or predict a failure mode.

Example of PM and PdM Using Roller Element Bearings:

Each of the different causes of bearing failure (failure mode) produces its own characteristic damage. Such damage, known as *primary damage*, gives rise to *secondary damage* (failure inducing), namely flaking and cracks. Even the primary damage may necessitate scrapping the bearings on account of excessive internal clearance, vibration, noise, and so on. A failed bearing frequently displays a combination of primary and secondary damage.

Figure 7-5: Example of Roller Element Bearing Failure

Primary Damage (or Failure Mode) for Roller Element Bearings

Wear: If there is not sufficient lubricant, or if the lubricant has lost its lubricating properties, it is not possible for an oil film with sufficient load carrying capacity to form. Metal-to-metal contact occurs between rolling elements and raceways.

The two maintenance strategies listed below need to be applied:

   a. Effective lubrication (the correct contaminant free lubricant applied in the correct amount at the correct time interval) is the most effective maintenance strategy to prevent catastrophic failure.

   b. Vibration analysis is the most effective maintenance strategy to identify the defect early enough so that the bearing can be replaced before catastrophic damage occurs.

Indentations: Raceways and rolling elements may become dented. If the mounting pressure is applied to the wrong ring (installed improperly), so that it passes through the rolling elements, or if the bearing is subjected to abnormal loading while not running, indentations will occur. Foreign particles in the bearing also cause indentations. Vibration analysis is an effective method for finding indentation defects caused by improper installation or storage.

The three maintenance strategies listed below need to be applied:

   a. Proper installation practices using effective work procedures is one effective maintenance strategy to prevent catastrophic failure.

b. Effective lubrication (contamination free lubrication) is one effective maintenance strategy to prevent catastrophic failure.
   c. Vibration analysis is the most effective maintenance strategy to identify the defect early enough so it can be replaced before catastrophic damage occurs.

Smearing: When two inadequately lubricated surfaces slide against each other under load, material is transferred from one surface to the other.

The three maintenance strategies listed below need to be applied:
   a. Proper installation practices using effective work procedures is one effective maintenance strategy to prevent catastrophic failure.
   b. Effective lubrication (contamination free lubrication) is one effective maintenance strategy to prevent catastrophic failure.
   c. Vibration analysis is the most effective maintenance strategy to identify the defect early enough so it can be replaced before catastrophic damage occurs.

Surface distress: If the lubricant film between raceways and rolling elements becomes too thin, the peaks of the surface asperities will momentarily come into contact with each other. Small cracks then form in the surfaces. Forming of these cracks is known as surface distress.

The three maintenance strategies listed below need to be applied:
   a. Effective lubrication (ensuring new equipment lubrication is compatible with your lubrication) is one effective maintenance strategy to prevent catastrophic failure.
   b. Effective lubrication (ensuring equipment which has a back-up is run on specific intervals to keep lubrication from being lost at point of startup) is one effective maintenance strategy to prevent catastrophic failure.
   c. Vibration analysis is the most effective maintenance strategy to identify the defect early enough so it can be replaced before catastrophic damage occurs.

Corrosion: Rust will form if water or corrosive agents reach the inside of the bearing in such quantities that the lubricant cannot provide protection for the steel surfaces.

FRACAS

The two maintenance strategies listed below need to be applied:

a. Effective lubrication (ensuring the lubrication is effective against moisture) is one effective maintenance strategy to prevent catastrophic failure.

b. Vibration analysis is the most effective maintenance strategy to identify the defect early enough so it can be replaced before catastrophic damage occurs.

Electric current damage: When an electric current passes through a bearing, i.e. proceeds from one ring to the other via the rolling elements, damage will occur. At the contact surfaces, the process is similar to electric arc welding.

The two maintenance strategies listed below need to be applied:

a. Ensuring welding grounds are within six inches of the welded surface is a maintenance strategy to prevent catastrophic failure.

b. Vibration analysis is the most effective maintenance strategy to identify the defect early enough so it can be replaced before catastrophic damage occurs.

Secondary Damage or Failure Mode for a Rolling Element Bearing

These defects—flaking and cracks—will not occur if one prevents or predicts the primary failure modes early enough.

The most interesting point the above example makes is that the use of multiple maintenance strategies must be used to prevent or predict specific failure modes.

Lessons learned from Preventive and Predictive Maintenance

Many lessons have been learned from the use of Preventive and Predictive Maintenance to address failure modes effectively:

- In order to identify and eliminate the cause of equipment failure, one will need to ensure accurate data is input into their CMMS/EAM. This data includes part–defect–cause. FRACAS cannot work without this lesson being applied in your organization.

- Multiple maintenance strategies need to be applied to specific components in order to prevent or predict specific failure modes.

- The Law of Diminishing Returns states that production output and the amount of preventive maintenance must be aligned to each other. Clearly there is a point at which increasing PM hurts the bottom line. The reason? Simple: most PM procedures require that the equipment is shut down. That means uptime goes down, so production output eventually goes down, too. Meanwhile, maintenance costs go up.

  So how much preventive maintenance is too much? According to a private study, the best practice programs generate 15% of their maintenance work from PM inspections. Another 15% is corrective work identified by those inspections.

- By definition, all PMs are time based. That means either calendar time or operating time dictates when an asset should be inspected, cleaned, adjusted, replaced or reconditioned. But is there really a direct relationship between the time equipment spends in service and the likelihood it will fail? In short, the answer is no. The truth is, most equipment failures are not age related. In fact, for complex systems, the majority of failures will occur at random.

  Consider the facts. In the Nowlan and Heap study, failure probabilities relative to the age of the equipment itself were low. Let's remember this study comes from the airline industry, where maintenance and operations standards are exceptionally high. That gives us a true picture of how equipment fails when it is maintained and operated correctly. The reality is, 89% of equipment failures are not age related. Therefore, there is no amount of time-based preventive maintenance that can manage these failures effectively.

  That's why using time as the primary basis for your maintenance strategy is inherently flawed. It will have very little impact on overall reliability. From a risk standpoint, it is much safer to assume that equipment failures can happen at any time.

- Reliability is a long-term investment strategy. It is not the place for turning a quick buck. Do not expect PM or PdM to provide immediate results. It is an investment.

Example of Failure to Perform Effective Maintenance Strategy

BP budgeted some $71 million for battling corrosion in its Alaskan pipelines in 2006. That is 15% more than in 2005, and 80% over 2001. And that doesn't include money for replacement and repairs. Was it enough? Apparently not; after the shutdown, **BP admitted inadequate pipeline maintenance procedures and "a gap" in their corrosion program.** The maintenance strategy was in place, however these strategies were not followed.

> *"We based our corrosion program in cooperation with agencies— what we thought was an adequate program. Clearly it was not."*
> – Bob Malone, President of BP America

> *"Our program was insufficient and will be rectified going forward."*
> – Steve Marshall, President of BP Alaska

Let's do the math. In essence, **BP was spending $71 million to protect an asset that delivers about $10 billion in annual revenues**. Now even if you don't know anything about maintenance and reliability, doesn't that sound a little risky?

Shortchanging maintenance is like playing Russian roulette—*pay now or pay later*.

- Inspecting equipment while it is running is better than inspecting it in a failure mode when it is down. A good example is a V-Belt. Inspecting it while it is down takes away time from the mechanic and from the operation of the equipment If one were to use a strobe light, a maintenance mechanic or operator would know if the belt is loose. If a belt is loose, it is much cheaper, in most cases, to change it out when found using the strobe light rather than inspecting and retensioning a V-Belt which is already beginning to fail, because when a belt loosens it is typically because the belt was beginning to fail.

STEP 5: Executing the Proactive Work from the Maintenance Strategies

Figure 7-6: Proactive Work

Maintenance Planning

A properly designed and executed maintenance planning process can be one of the most effective means available to aid in the elimination of failures by ensuring that the daily execution of maintenance activities are repeatable using effective/repeatable procedures, standards, specifications, and the right parts.

The purpose of any planning process should be to eliminate delays in the maintenance process so the maintenance work can be executed according to schedule. This will provide maintenance the time to conduct the maintenance activity at a speed at which the quality of the end result is not jeopardized. When planning is not effective, maintenance personnel are standing around or running to find parts and thus direct labor is higher. A reactive organization will typically have a wrench time of 2%–30% (I have seen much lower numbers) where best in class is 55% plus. (I have numbers as high as 65%.) View Figure 7-7 for an example of the percentage of time consumed with common delays.

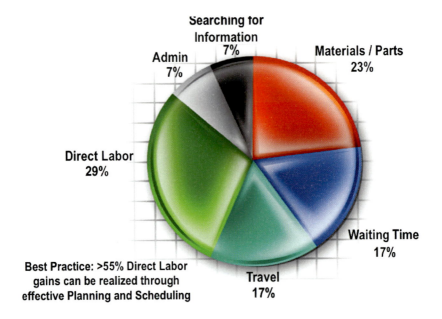

Figure 7-7: Common Delays Caused by Lack of Effective Planning

Not all jobs are good candidates for planning. Very simple jobs do not have much value that can be added via planning, so they normally would not go through the planning process. This practice frees the planner up to focus on jobs where planning can leverage his time by two- or even threefold. Every organization involved in maintenance planning management should identify the jobs that should not be planned. However, all jobs are good candidates for scheduling as long as a reasonable time estimate can be made. The key is that maintenance planners should never be involved in emergency or urgent work.

In general, the planner identifies everything that will be needed to execute the job. As maintenance work requests are made from the operating or maintenance department, it should be a continual process for them to be "funneled" through the maintenance supervisor for verification as to which work is planned or not.

The planner is next in line to receive the work request once the maintenance supervisor has performed his/her review. The planner's most important role is to identify and quantify the resources that will be required to execute a given job. Categorically, these resources are:

1. Number of maintenance personnel and man-hours required for skill level and crafts required.
2. Steps required to complete the job.
3. Part needs.
4. Tool and equipment needs.
5. Information needs including drawings and specifications.

In so doing, planning prevents most delays from materializing and thereby greatly improves maintenance effectiveness. The planner is usually one of the best craftsmen who also has the additional skills of excellent written communication, information management, computer skills, managing multiple priorities, and is methodical and well organized, to name a few.

The planner will review the work requests to see that they are written on the correct equipment in the CMMS, otherwise correct them and then determine if he will need to do a field visit or not. The planner should conduct a field visit on any work that is not obviously routine and straightforward. During a job site inspection, the planner will identify the resources required by the job and also note ancillary repairs/equipment needs that should be resolved during work order execution. Any other delays that are likely to be present will also be noted. Sources of other delays can be: 1) job preparation; 2) permits; 3) lockout/tag out; and 4) physical access problems, to name a few. The planner will determine how best to prevent each identified delay from materializing and take the steps necessary to prevent the delay. For example, a job may have very difficult access that scaffolding could resolve; the planner identifies the need for scaffolding and gives an estimate of the time that would be required to erect the scaffolding. All of this information will be documented in a standardized form called a Job Plan for each planned work order. In this example, when the job came up to be scheduled, the need for scaffolding would be recognized, and the job would be scheduled allowing sufficient time for the assembly of the scaffolding. If the planner believes that a particular job is likely to be repeated again and again in the future, he will likely store the plan, thus cutting the time required for him to process similar work orders in the future

Job status codes are used throughout the P&S (Planning and Scheduling) process to segregate work into its various stages as it progresses through the process. Common status categories are:

- In Planning (number of work orders)
- Awaiting Parts (labor hours)
- Waiting for Approval (labor hours)
- On Hold (labor hours)
- Ready to be Scheduled – Planning Complete (labor hours)
- Backlog (measured in weeks or labor hours)

The planner normally reserves parts that will be needed for jobs and places orders for any that will come from off the plant site. Once the job plan is complete and all part needs have been resolved, meaning that they can be available in less than 24 hours, the job will be coded as "Ready to be Scheduled," signifying that the planning phase is now complete. The on-site parts will actually be ordered and all required parts put in a kit a day or two before the date the job is scheduled to start.

The job will now go to maintenance scheduling.

Maintenance Scheduling

A Maintenance Scheduler or Planner/Scheduler optimizes production needs and schedules according to the availability and capacity of the maintenance resources. Different organizations use different strategies; some use weekly schedules only, some only daily schedules, and still others use both. The nuances of these various strategies are beyond the scope of this chapter, so we will just assume that a schedule is created and communicated to all parties.

A common problem reported by reliability professionals is that too often, preventive maintenance work and corrective maintenance work identified by predictive technologies linger in the maintenance backlog unattended until a failure develops. You hear management ask the common reactive question, "How much more will it run?" The scheduling process presents another opportunity to aid reliability and prevent this malady.

This is a real story of the real cost of unreliability:

On a Thursday afternoon, an industrial facility's management team begins looking at a motor in the final stages of failure.

Steps to Implementing an Effective FRACAS

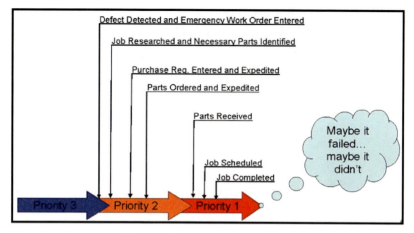

Figure 7-9: Reactive Work

FRACAS will require a planner/scheduler or planners and schedulers to ensure the right data is on all work orders when opened, planned, and scheduled or used for reactive maintenance (breakdown). They must ensure the following data is accurate 100% of the time:

- ➢ Equipment number
- ➢ Work order description
- ➢ Work order type
- ➢ Total hours by craft
- ➢ Cost (labor, material, contractor, etc.)
- ➢ Follow-up work identified
- ➢ On PMs, there must be quantitative measures in order to identify the defect severity.

FRACAS requires a maintenance or reliability engineer, PdM technician, or skilled maintenance technician to enter the part-defect-cause for every repair. The maintenance supervisor should validate all of this information before the work order is closed out.

Maintenance Execution

Executing maintenance, whether preventive maintenance, predictive maintenance, planned repairs, installation of new equipment, emergency or urgent work, all require the same ingredients to ensure a reliable, failure-free operation:

- Discipline in work execution.
- Making repairs to standard following repeatable procedures.
- Proper recording of findings and actions.
- Lessons learned.
- Work-order data is accurate.
- Make change recommendations for any procedure, specification, or standard. If changes are made, the MOC (Management of Change) process must be followed.
- Commissioning of equipment if a repair, replacement, or installation of a new part, equipment, etc. is executed. (Commissioning many times involves predictive technology to ensure no defect is identified after one of the above is completed.)

FRACAS (Failure Reporting, Analysis, and Corrective Action System)

Once the maintenance strategy is developed and implemented, continuous improvements on the strategy should take place. Sometimes this is referred to as Failure Reporting, Analysis, and Corrective Action System (FRACAS). An easy way to think of FRACAS is the following, Figure 7-10:

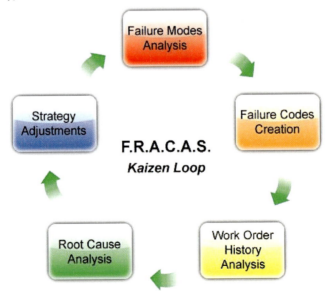

Figure 7-10: FRACAS Loop

Failure Modes Analysis

This block represents the entire EMP (Equipment Maintenance Plan) Analysis which identifies all known failure modes that are expected to occur. Three processes can be used: Reliability-Centered Maintenance, Failure Modes and Effect Analysis, or Failure Modes Mapping. Use of all three strategies is recommended once you have ranked all your assets based on criticality.

Failure Codes Creation

The Failure Codes (Defect) in a Computerized Maintenance Management System (CMMS) should match very closely, if not verbatim, to the failure modes listed in the failure modes library. This makes the next block much more powerful.

Work Order History Analysis

One of the roles of the reliability engineer is to periodically (best practice = monthly) analyze the failures that have occurred in the plant and compare those failures to the failure modes library. Do the failures that have occurred match up with the failures that were expected? If not, why not?

Root Cause Analysis

Root Cause Analysis is used when one requires knowing the true root cause of a repeatable failure or one which resulted in specific losses. Once the root cause has been established, one of a few things must happen:

1. The maintenance strategy must be adjusted or changed based on the results. A preventive maintenance procedure may need to be modified, changed completely, or predictive maintenance may be used because it detects potential failures before they become functional failures.

2. The equipment may require a redesign to eliminate this failure. A good example would be a hydraulic pump failure due to contamination of the fluid (see Figure 7-11). A redesign would require a modification to the reservoir, a filter pump to install oil into the reservoir, and a more effective storage area for the hydraulic fluid.

FRACAS

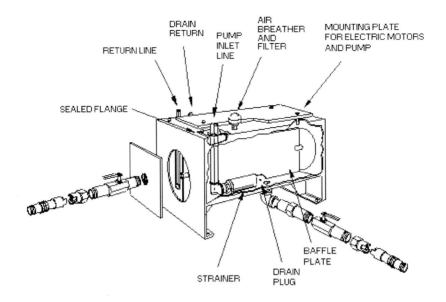

Figure 7-11: Hydraulic System Redesign

Strategy Adjustments – Earlier we discussed what a maintenance strategy is and found the following:

A maintenance strategy is a prescriptive plan to protect equipment from failure by identifying the best solution for specific equipment which results in optimized reliability at optimal cost. Less invasive is preferred to more invasive. This is one of the fundamental concepts of any well-defined maintenance strategy. Specific maintenance strategies are designed to mitigate the consequences of each failure mode. As a result, maintenance is viewed as a reliability function instead of a repair function. Saying this means Predictive Maintenance or Condition Monitoring is the best solution because it is mainly noninvasive.

With this being the definition, one may ask, "Why am I adjusting the current PM or PdM strategy?" FRACAS is your continuous improvement loop and if a maintenance strategy is not effective, then it must be reviewed and adjusted as needed.

Defining Roles and Responsibilities for FRACAS

The RACI chart is used when defining who is Responsible, Accountable, Consulted, and Informed during the execution and management of the FRACAS process.

RACI is a chart used by many of the largest and most successful corporations in the world to ensure all employees know their roles and responsibilities in any process that is to be managed and executed in a disciplined manner. In Figure 7-12, you will see an example of a RACI chart applied to the FRACAS process.

FRACAS RACI Chart
FRACAS Continuous Improvement and Defect Elimination Process

Tasks	Maintenance Supervisors	Maintenance Planner	Maintenance Technician	Maintenance Manager	Reliability Engineer	PdM Technician
Inputting Failure Data - CMMS/EAM	A	I	R		C	C
Work Order Close Out	R	C	R	A	R	R
Validating Failure Data and Codes	C	I	C	A	R	C
QA of Failure Data Input	I	C		A	R	C
Analyze Failure Reports	R	I	C	R	A/R	R
Making Maintenance Strategy Adjustments	I	I	I	A	R	C

Responsibility — "the Doer"
Accountable — "the Buck stops here"
Consulted — "in the Loop"
Informed — "kept in the picture"

Figure 7-12: RACI Chart

RACI charting is a technique for identifying functional areas, key activities, and decision points where ambiguities exist. With RACI, differences can be brought into the open and resolved through a team effort.

This approach enables management to participate in the process of describing activities, making decisions at specific points, and clarifying the responsibilities of each person in the failure reporting process.

A few general rules used in this methodology include:

- Place Accountability (A) and Responsibility (R) to the level closest to the action or knowledge.
- Only one person can be accountable.
- Authority must accompany accountability.

- Minimize Consultants (C) and Informs (I).
- If more than two are Responsible (R), then the activity or decision needs to be broken down into more parts.
- Decisions made in RACI charting must be accomplished with all team players.
- Responsible (R) is defined as the "doers."
- Accountable (A) is defined as "the buck stops here."
- Consulted (C) is defined as" who needs to be consulted on a specific activity or decision (two-way communication)."
- Informed (I) is defined as "keeping in the loop" (one-way communication).
- Ensure all roles and responsibilities are addressed.

In conclusion, the RACI model is a great method to ensure a failure reporting process is followed and everyone knows their role, which contributes to success.

References:

Smith, Ricky, "Reliability 101 Workshop Session," GPAllied, 2009.

Page, Andy, "Developing Effective Workshop Series," GPAllied, 2007.

Gehloff, Mike, "Planning and Scheduling Workshop Series," GPAllied 2009.

Page, Andy, "Introduction to Condition Monitoring," Allied Reliability 2007.

Page, Andy, "Developing Effective Workshop Series," GPAllied, 2009.

Smith, Ricky, and Mobley, Keith, *Industrial Machinery Repair: Best Maintenance Practices,* Elsevier Publishing, 2004.

CHAPTER 8

The Cost of Unreliability

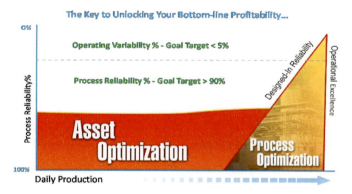

Figure 8-1: Transformational Analytics Plots

The cost of unreliability many times goes truly unknown because the causes of unreliability are many. Equipment failures need to be monetized in order for management to understand the true losses which exist in a company.

Whether you want to point the finger at maintenance, production (operations), or engineering, each functional area plays a role in unreliability and the true losses incurred by equipment failures. If a company cannot identify their losses, they will lose their business to inside or outside competition and these people will lose their jobs. An inside competitor is another operation in your company which produces or performs the same function. An outside competitor is a company who wants your business and will take it from you if one does not truly know the losses incurred.

The Market Survivor Model

We know through benchmarking data that financial losses due to equipment failures are known for dividing the winners from the losers. A winner knows what the cost of unreliability is, and the loser does not until they lose some or all of their business to an inside competitor, or an outside one. If you were to identify your organization in the Market Survivor Model (Figure 8-2), which was developed by Ron Moore of the RM Group, you will find where your organization truly stands in regards to being successful and sustaining. For company "C," they have a small amount of the market share, and typically this company incurs the highest cost per unit produced. Company "B" has a larger portion of market share, however their cost per unit produced is higher than company "A." Company "A" will typically have less equipment failures due to operator, maintenance, and engineering issues. In order for your company to survive you want to be in the position of company "A."

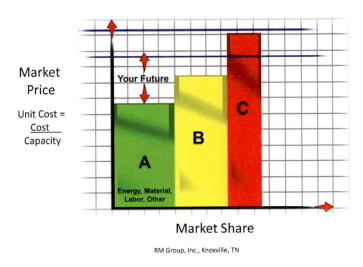

Figure 8-2: Market Survivor Model

You may be thinking that failures do not account for all losses in an organization and this is true; however, if you take into account all functional failures (and their financial impact) from production, maintenance, and engineering, you will find the majority of financial losses are from failures.

Example Number One of Unreliability

A good example of the cost of unreliability would be a true experience with a production facility whose true name I will not reveal. A few numbers are changed to protect the innocent. This facility had been in operation for over thirty years and had seen profit for most of those years. A financial analysis (business case for change) was performed to determine what the true value was, in what we call the "hidden plant." The results revealed the following:

- $7.6 million in savings could be returned to the owners in 6 months from both maintenance and production.
- A new $12 million expansion could be stopped because of the hidden capacity revealed in this plant.
- Over 90% of the financial gain would come from the elimination of specific functional failures.

The plant did not move forward with the initiative thus resulting in losses of jobs within one year to an outside competitor. The plant shut the doors within three years due to inside competition. One of their sister plants produced the same product at a much lower cost.

Example Number Two of Unreliability – Different Context

The U.S. Army Corp of Engineers builds all the buildings in the world for the U.S. Army, so the U.S. Army is happy when the U.S. Army Corp of Engineers gives the Army a one-year warranty for anything in a new facility. Think about a large horsepower motor. How long should it run without a problem? Ten years? Twenty years? If it is installed improperly and defect is present upon startup, then it will last just over one year, even if the contractor used a straight edge to align the motor shaft. I want twenty years of failure-free service, and if equipment was validated upon commissioning, by using predictive technology, we would know if a defect is present when the equipment starts up. A defect is an abnormality in a component which leads to equipment or asset failure. The I-P-F curve illustrates (as shown in Figure 8-3) the timing of the defect. Will you detect it in time? Why not ensure there are no defects when a new part, repair, or a new asset is installed effectively?

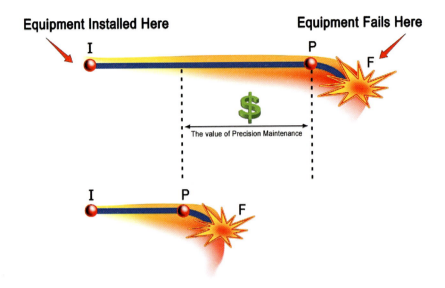

Figure 8-3: I-P-F Curve

If a "soft foot" (a "soft foot" is an out-of-plane condition typically on one motor foot) is not identified upon commissioning, will it cause a premature failure with 100% certainty? A defect has started the decline of reliability of the asset, and failure will occur unless the defect is detected early enough and repaired properly. (Of course we need time to properly plan and schedule the work.) If the U.S. Army Corp of Engineers spends billions of U.S. dollars in new facilities a year, then how much would unreliability cost the tax payers? Could this be happening to you on a smaller scale?

Maintenance Cost Reduction

The reduction of maintenance cost is known output reliability so unreliability causes an increase in maintenance. The following chart was developed based on a survey that shows that as a company moves from a reactive to a proactive model, the cost of maintaining reliability goes down (see Figure 8-4). Thomas Marketing completed this research in 1997, however, AT Kearney found basically the same results in 1992, as did the Aberdeen Group in 2008. If you optimize the maintenance process, you will reduce cost and increase asset reliability. The goal being optimal asset reliability at optimal cost.

The Cost of Unreliability

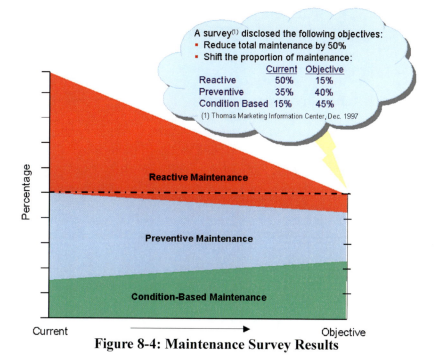

Figure 8-4: Maintenance Survey Results

Building a Reliable Organization
(Optimal reliability at optimal cost)

Eliminating unreliability (see Figure 8-5) illustrates the functions required in order to move from a reactive to a proactive maintenance program.

> *"You cannot have continuous improvement until you have a sustainable process."* – Unknown

Figure 8-5: Reliability Organization

FRACAS

The elimination of failures with continuous improvement built in, however, cannot be successful without the all the different functions in place for its success. Reliability improvements will only be implemented when a solid FRACAS is in place.

Managing Reliability or Asset Health

Asset health can be affected by many sources which create defects that are abnormalities in part, and lead to equipment or asset failure if not corrected in time. A defect comes from two different sources.

One source of defects comes from people, and the other comes from how they deal with the machinery. As people work on machines, they sometimes create defects. Some examples are:

- The shafts were not aligned to standard before operating a motor.
- Pipe stress on a pump is not identified.
- The motor is not lubricated with the correct grease. Motor came with petroleum-based grease, and now the mechanic mixes synthetic grease into the motor.
- Start-up procedure is not effective or does not match reality.
- Machine is overloaded, or over sped during production.

All of these cause defects, and they have everything to do with how we interact with the machine. We will refer to these as *systemic problems*. The system referred to is the man-machine system. The impact of systemic problems is easily seen in the I-P-F curve. The I-P-F curve is the standard PF curve with the I-P portion added as seen in Figure 8-6.

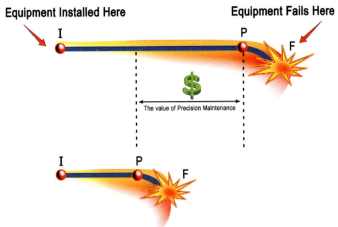

Figure 8-6: The I-P-F Curve

Point I is defined as the point of installation of the component. The I-P portion of the I-P-F curve is the failure-free period. This is the time during which the operation is defect free. On machines that were installed improperly, this may be just a few seconds. On machines that were installed and/or repaired properly, this may be years. The graphic shows what the I-P-F curve for two identical machines might look like. One machine was installed using precision measuring devices and well-trained crafts personnel operating with a properly designed procedure. The other machine was installed by inadequately trained personnel who were not using precision instruments or techniques and had no procedure to follow. The difference in lengths of the I-P portions of the curve can be easily conveyed in dollars. The dollars represent the additional cost of parts and labor and also the cost of additional foregone production as a result of the extra maintenance work that had to be performed. An excellent way to determine the maturity of the maintenance effort is not by looking at the age of the program but by where their focus is on the I-P-F curve.

An organization that is constantly focused on point F and staying clear of it, will undoubtedly be a reactive culture. Typical things heard around this organization might be "How long can we run it before it fails?" and "Just how bad is it?"

First, as the organization matures, the focus shifts from point F to point P. The organization then focuses its efforts on understanding how things fail and their ability to detect these failures early. Typical things overheard in this organization may be something like "Is this the best way to detect these defects early?" or "I appreciate you letting me know about this problem, even though it's very early."

Then, another transition is made from the focus on point P to a focus on point I. Overheard in the hallways of this organization are things like "Leaking roof was repaired using no procedure or skilled person (the roof had been repaired many times)." The manager should make this statement: "Let's update the procedures for that job to reflect what we just learned." This organization is trying to prevent failures from ever occurring in the first place by applying best practices with fits, tolerances, alignment standards, contamination control and well-documented procedures. They are the ones who will see the step change in performance, and they are the ones we label "mature"; *not* the organization that has been doing it poorly but for a longer period of time.

FRACAS

Second, there are the defects that stem from the operating environment or the operating context. These defects are the result of the environment in which the machine operates. Some examples are:

- Overhead crane gearboxes in plants located in hot regions of the United States will see drastically hotter temperatures in the summer than the same gearbox in Wisconsin. As a result, lubrication problems may be much more prevalent.
- Motors operating in a dusty environment, such as inside a building where carbon is produced, are much more likely to have their cooling fins clogged than a motor operating a freshwater pump down by the river.
- Pumps that have to change speeds to constantly adjust flow characteristics to account for system adjustments are much more likely to run with flow turbulence issues, like cavitations, than a pump that never has to change speeds and has a constant inlet and outlet pressure.
- Electrical equipment that sees constant changes in load are more likely to develop thermal anomalies or hot spots as a result of the heating-up and cooling-down process than electrical equipment that sees much more stable loads.
- Motors that are constantly starting under high load conditions, or motors that experience large variations in load during normal operations, are much more prone to rotor bar defects, than motors that run all the time and at the same load.

These are a few examples of how operating context can be a source of defects. We will refer to these as *operating envelope problems*.

Both systemic problems and operating envelope problems manifest themselves in the same way as specific component or part level defects. Some examples are:

- Rolling element defects
- Gear defects
- Contaminated lubricant
- Loose/dirty electrical connections
- Shorted motor windings

Knowing that both systemic problems and operating envelope problems produce the same type of defects, a maintenance strategy that merely attempts to discover the defects and correct them will never be able to reach a proactive state. Technicians will be too busy fixing the symptoms of problems instead of addressing the root cause.

To reach a truly proactive state, the root cause of the defects will need to be identified and eliminated. Maintenance strategies that accomplish this are able to see the step change in performance and achieve incredible cost savings.

Maintenance strategies that do not attempt to address the root cause of defects will continue to see lackluster results and struggle with financial performance. Another way to maintain focus on identifying and eliminating the root cause of the problem is to focus on the defect, and not the failure.

Nowlan and Heap Report on Reliability

The Nowlan and Heap released reliability report of 1978 resulted in a few significant findings, which are applicable in most organizations today and can be applied to eliminate failures. These include:

- There are essentially only four types of tasks in a scheduled maintenance program. Maintenance personnel can be asked to:

    a. Inspect an item to detect a potential failure.

    b. Rework an item before a maximum permissible age is exceeded.

    c. Discard an item before a maximum permissible age is exceeded.

    d. Inspect an item to find failures that have already occurred but were not evident to the equipment operating crew.

- A complex asset, whose functional failure may result from many different failure modes, shows little or no decrease in overall reliability with increasing age unless there is a dominant failure mode. Age limits imposed on complex assets, components, and systems (including the equipment itself) therefore have little or no effect on their overall failure rates.

- Many types of failures cannot be prevented, no matter how intensive the scheduled maintenance activities.

In conclusion, if we look at the failure patterns (Figure 8-7) which resulted from this study you will find that 89% of failures are random and thus require predictive technology to identify the failure far

FRACAS

enough in advance to plan and schedule corrective work effectively. These identical failure patterns have shown up with similar results in other organizations who have conducted similar studies. The cost of unreliability is high because most companies try to use preventive maintenance as their primary driver to reduce failures, and do not use predictive maintenance effectively to identify a defect (when a failure begins) in an asset far enough in advance so work can be planned and scheduled effectively without resulting in losses due to scheduled and unscheduled maintenance.

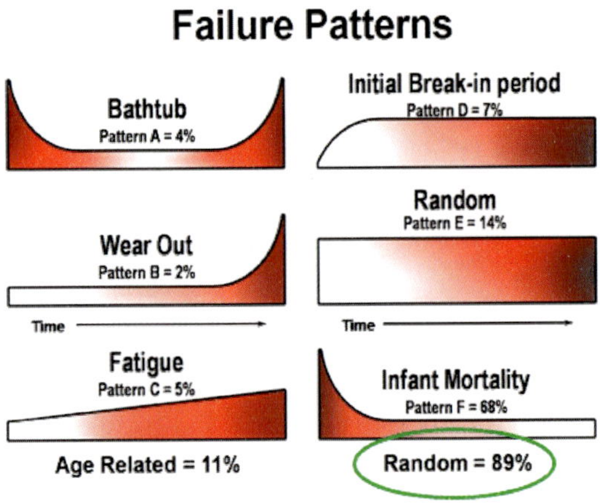

Failure Patterns

- Bathtub — Pattern A = 4%
- Wear Out — Pattern B = 2%
- Fatigue — Pattern C = 5%
- Initial Break-in period — Pattern D = 7%
- Random — Pattern E = 14%
- Infant Mortality — Pattern F = 68%

Age Related = 11%   Random = 89%

Figure 8-7: Failure Patterns

Conclusion

In the world of maintenance and reliability, most companies spend too much money for the reliability they receive. It is not their fault. The saying is: "You don't know what you don't know."

References

Transformational Analytics Plots, GPAllied, 2009.

Moore, Ron, RM Group, Knoxville, TN.

Page, Andy, and Schultz, John, "PdM Secrets Document," GPAllied, 2008.

Maintenance Survey Results, Thomas Marketing Information Center, 2007.

Nowlan, F. Stanley, and Heap, Howard F., *Reliability-Centered Maintenance*, Department of Defense Report Number A066-579, December 29, 1978.

CHAPTER 9

Managing Change in a Failure Elimination Organization

Figure 9-1: RCA Elements Guide

The Proactive Organization and Failure Elimination

The Failure Reporting, Analysis, and Corrective Action System is a continuous improvement approach that is enabled by an organization that is proactive. It assumes a maintenance process is in place with the appropriate mix of predictive maintenance and preventive inspections, identifying defects as close to P as possible AND a proactive workflow system that plans and schedules the work to not only eliminate the defects but to also lengthen the interval between installation (I) and where the defect first enters the system (P). A proactive organization is one that has time to spend identifying defects as close to P as possible, planning and scheduling work, and removing the defects. FRACAS is the continuous improvement of the failure elimination process that lessens the likelihood defects will enter the system.

What we do not consider in FRACAS is that the latent cause of most failures is human behavior which is shown in Figure 9-1 of the RCA Elements Guide. The difficulty begins when we interject the human element into FRACAS. Everyone wants to do what they have always done.

Characteristics of a Proactive Organization

A proactive organization has several characteristics. It can be identified by the integrated nature of its functions and how they are focused on and aligned to supporting the organization's mission, and optimizing customer satisfaction. This is generally measured by quality, quantity, and on-time delivery. For example, criticality of assets in a proactive organization is based on its impact on the system—the plant's ability to produce, rather than its function—and a department's ability to meet its performance goals.

The prevailing method of thinking, or mental model, in a proactive organization is based on "systems thinking." Everyone in the organization understands how his or her role directly or indirectly contributes to accomplishing the organization's mission, and how the function of the assets within the production system is interdependent on creating value for the customer. The culture in such an organization on Steven Covey's maturity continuum would be "interdependent," emphasizing more "we" than "me," where teams are self-directed and make decisions of import resulting in more proactive behavior. Directly the opposite is a "dependent" culture where control and decision making are taken from the workforce and directed toward what to do, thereby creating reactive behavior.

An example of these concepts is in the parable of the three men working in a rock quarry. The first man is asked what he is doing and he replies, "I am breaking big rocks into little rocks." The second man is asked the same question, and he replies, "I am earning a living to support my family and send my children to college so they don't have to work in a quarry." Finally, the third man is asked what he is doing and he replies, "I am building a cathedral." While all three answers are true from each individual perspective, a proactive organization strives for the third response as a purpose statement.

Peter Senge's research in *The Fifth Discipline* indicates that there are two motivators in an organization: fear and aspiration. It is the preferred method of leadership and organization design to leverage the latter for optimum performance; therefore our systems, structure, and leadership styles must be aligned to that end. To achieve a proactive organization with an interdependent culture, the "system"—as Deming called it—must be designed for the results.

The concept of a proactive organization is grounded in Deming's System of Profound Knowledge consisting of four parts that interact with one another and cannot be separated. They are: understanding of a system; knowledge of variation; theory of knowledge and; knowledge of psychology—the intrinsic motivation, vision and aspiration of individuals within an organization. The resultant of the organizational system is performance, and performance is the result of the organization's behavior or culture.

The three drivers of an organization's culture are its systems, structure, and style of leadership. How information is shared, how performance is measured and rewarded, how learning occurs, and how products are made would be examples of the organization's systems. The structure could be typified by how the organization is organized to control, to make decisions, and to execute work. Finally, the style of leadership is the level of control exercised by the supervisors. For example, a level of control such as "no work can be executed without a supervisor's approval" could result in a culture of dependency—people standing around waiting to be told what to do (usually accompanied by supervisors lamenting about the lack of initiative in the workforce).

Discipline

Discipline in an organization is the extent to which the workforce holds themselves accountable to following standards and procedures. The further the workforce performance varies from standard, the less the discipline is to maintain the standard. It is directly correlated to accountability. A good acid test for this is when asked the question, "Why are the people not following procedures?" is to ask another question: "What is allowing them to not follow procedures?" The answer to the second question would lie in one or more parts of the style of leadership, the organization's systems, and the organization's structure which are all aligned to enable this behavior. As Deming has said, "Your system is perfectly designed to give you the results you are getting," so if we are getting results that are undesirable, "Blame the system and not the people."

To increase the likelihood people will follow procedures most of the time, they not only have to know the procedure, they have to understand why the procedure exists, and what its impact on the system will be if the procedure is done correctly versus incorrectly. They must also understand the impact on their own lives when the procedure is done correctly versus incorrectly, as well as what their role is in executing the procedure. They must also have the knowledge and ability to follow the procedures. Finally, there must be a system for measuring variation from standard, and a system of accountability to reinforce desirable behaviors. Any time a change is made within an organization—such as implementing FRACAS—the system, structure, and leadership style must be realigned to reinforce the new way of thinking and behaving. Otherwise, the result might end up as the definition of insanity: "Continuing to do things the same way and expecting different results." – Albert Einstein

Discipline and Failure Elimination

Failure elimination relies on data gathering, analysis of that data, and taking actions to eliminate failures or mitigate the impact of those failures. FRACAS is a systemic approach to improving failure elimination. The process steps for FRACAS are:

1. Failure investigation.
2. Closing work orders with proper codes.
3. Analysis of work order history .
4. Planning and executing actions to correct system deficiencies identified during analysis .
5. Changing procedures to eliminate repeat of the same defects.

In establishing a FRACAS, a reactive organization would first start their journey to becoming proactive by doing a "bad actor" analysis, and then begin fixing the assets causing the most headaches. This is a good way to start, but it is a point solution as it focuses at the machine level instead of the system level, and misses many common cause issues. Using an aluminum smelter as an example, the Green Mill has a total of 41 asset failures. Several of these assets are "bad actors," and an effort is made to repair them to remove the pain. This isn't enough information for any proactive analysis and response to eliminate failures, so further investigation reveals the Number 2 Press had 17 failures. Digging deeper, it is discovered the motor for the Number 2 press had 11 failures. This information is still not granular enough to identify opportunities for failure elimination, so more historical data is needed. It is learned that 7 of the 11 motor failures were the result of bearing failures; 1 due to misalignment and 6 due to lubrication. The key suspect for further failure investigation and elimination now appears to be lubrication, and a Root Cause Analysis can determine actions to change procedures to eliminate the defects causing the lubrication failures, thus having the greatest impact on asset health.

This example describes a systematic approach that requires a new way of thinking, behaving, and discipline to follow through.

Implementing Discipline

> *"If there is a problem with performance, blame the system and not the people."*
>
> *"Your system is perfectly designed to give you the results you are getting."*
>
> *"Ninety percent of an organization's problems are created by management."*
>
> – Dr. Deming

The implementation of discipline in an organization has the following five requirements:

1. Clearly defined performance expectations.
2. Clearly defined boundaries of accountability and responsibility.
3. Training to provide the knowledge and skills to execute the performance expectations to an acceptable level.
4. A system for measuring key performance indicators.

5. A system of accountability to reinforce desired behaviors and provide consequences for undesirable behaviors.

These are the system components of an organization that will enable discipline.

Organization (from the root word "organic") could be defined as an entity made up of living beings assembled to accomplish a common mission. Using an outside-in approach, the executive leadership monitors the environment for opportunities and threats and sets vision, mission, and values for the organization. They next establish a strategic goal for the organization to accomplish, usually along the lines of happy customers, happy stockholders, happy employees, and a happy community.

The executive leadership now determines the organization's structure to execute work and installs enabling systems through human resources, finances, logistics, information technology, etc. They then assign leaders to accomplish the functional goals on which they are measured and rewarded. These three elements working in concert create the "culture" of the organization, that is, what members think, how they behave, what they value, and what they teach to newcomers.

If there is a performance issue, such as lack of discipline, the first step is to determine what part of the system is at fault. Are expectations clearly defined? Is responsibility and accountability understood? Do people know how to do their job? Are they measured on their work output and held accountable to results? If they are unable to achieve target performance levels, are system obstacles addressed and removed? If the answer to all of these issues is "yes," then the issue is motivation, and discipline is the appropriate response. If the answer to any one of these questions is "no," then the issue is "systemic" and must be resolved by the managers who control the systems. Simply telling someone to do something will not guarantee the discipline to do it. Telling them louder will not do it, and using fear as a motivator will not do it in any reliable and sustainable fashion. It must combine the intrinsic desire of individuals to do the right thing and the organization's systems, structure, and leadership style to reinforce that attitude.

Do not underestimate training and communication. As we learn from Ken Blanchard's research, knowledge precedes attitude and attitude drives behavior. The workforce must be aware of and understand the new way of doing things and they must know how it will affect their lives, what their role is in making it happen, and what they are expected to do. Finally, they must have the knowledge, skill, and ability to implement, execute, and sustain the change.

CHAPTER 10

Seven Steps to a Working FRACAS

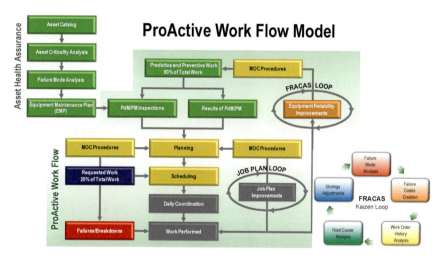

Figure 10-1: Proactive Maintenance with FRACAS for Equipment Reliability Improvements

Sustainable Change Is the Objective

You've gotten buy-in from the boss by showing him how much money the organization can make from a good FRACAS. He said, "Great idea! Now go make it happen." How many new ideas have you seen come and go in your organization? I have seen many through my career and I am sure you have as well. FRACAS is something that must be sustainable because it is the continuous improvement process for your Maintenance Strategies for each piece of equipment. In this chapter, we are going to offer you a phased approach to success, one step at a time.

- **FRACAS Step 1** – Determine your end goal.
  - Know where you are going.

- **FRACAS Step 2** – Create your data collection plan.
  - What measures will be used?
  - What data must be collected to create the measures?
  - How will the data be collected?
  - How will the data be analyzed?

- **FRACAS Step 3** – Determine organizational roles, goals, and responsibilities (RACI).
  - Who collects the data?
  - Who analyzes the data?
  - Who takes what action based on analysis results?

- **FRACAS Step 4** – Create the FRACAS Policies and Procedures Manual.
  - Create a manual that clearly delineates the items determined in Steps 1, 2, and 3.

- **FRACAS Step 5** – Develop and execute the FRACAS Training Plan.
  - Create a Training Plan based on the organizational roles, goals, and responsibilities determined in Step 3.

- **FRACAS Step 6** – Implement the FRACAS.
  - Hold required informational meetings.
  - Begin data collection on highest priority systems.
  - Analyze data and report results.
  - Create corrective actions based on results.

- **FRACAS Step 7** – Monitor and adjust.
  - Monitor data quality and results.
  - Monitor corrective actions.
  - Adjust data collection plan and corrective action implementation plan based on results of monitoring.

FRACAS Step 1 – Determine Your End Goal

"Would you tell me, please, which way I ought to go from here?"
"That depends a good deal on where you want to get to," said the Cat.
"I don't much care where—"said Alice.
"Then it doesn't matter which way you go," said the Cat.
"—so long as I get SOMEWHERE," Alice added as an explanation.
"Oh, you're sure to do that," said the Cat, "if you only walk long enough."

- *Alice's Adventures in Wonderland*, Chapter 6

The beginning of every journey starts with a destination. The beginning of the journey to an effective FRACAS is the same as any other. You must have an end goal in mind. The goal of a FRACAS is not to gather data, but to eliminate failures from the organization. Knowing this helps ensure that every policy, procedure, and activity in the system is goal oriented. The roles, goals, and responsibilities of everyone involved with the system can be focused toward that goal. Having the goal in mind allows you to build the shared vision and values that will make the system work successfully for you.

FRACAS Step 2 – Create the Data Collection Plan

There are four steps to create the data collection plan:

1. Determine the measures you will use.

    There are a number of activities associated with the implementation of a good FRACAS. Measures need to be created that help you determine whether or not activities are being done, and whether or not the activities are being effective at eliminating failures. Some suggested measures are listed here, but this list should not be considered all inclusive. It is best to create a set of measures that fit the needs of your organization.

    - **Mean Time Between Failures (MTBF)** – MTBF is the arithmetic average of the individual times to failure. FRACAS activities should drive MTBF up.
        - $MTBF = \sum_{i=1}^{N} \frac{TTF_i}{N}$
    - **Mean Time to Repair (MTTR)** – MTTR is the arithmetic average of the individual times to repair. FRACAS activities should drive MTTR down.
        - $MTTR = \sum_{i=1}^{N} \frac{TTR_i}{N}$

- **Availability (A)** – A is the percent of time that equipment is available to perform its required function. FRACAS activities should drive A up.
  - $A = \dfrac{MTBF}{MTBF + MTTR}$
- **Cost per Failure**
- **Type of Failure** (Wearout, Fatigue, Random, etc. based on the six patterns identified by Nowlan and Heap's team)
- **Number of RCAs Ordered based on System Triggers**
- **Percent of RCAs Completed** –
  - $RCA\ Completion\ Percentage = \left(\dfrac{RCAs\ Completed}{RCAs\ Ordered}\right) \times 100$
- **Number of Corrective Actions Recommended**
- **Percent of Corrective Actions Approved (%PCA)**
  - $\%PCA = \left(\dfrac{Corrective\ Actions\ Approved}{Corrective\ Actions\ Recommended}\right) \times 100$
- **Percent of Corrective Actions Implemented (%PCI)**
  - $\%PCI = \left(\dfrac{Corrective\ Actions\ Implemented}{Corrective\ Actions\ Approved}\right) \times 100$
- **Corrective Action Effectiveness (CAE)**
  - $CAE = \left(\dfrac{Failures\ Eliminated}{Corrective\ Actions\ Implemented}\right) \times 100$

2. Determine what data needs to be collected to create the desired measures.

   The data that needs to be collected will be determined by the desired measures. The following table contains a list of some of the most basic data needed.

Table 10-1: Data Needed for Established Measures

DATA REQUIRED	REASON REQUIRED
Failure Data Information	
Date and Time of Part Installation	Used to determine Time to Failure for MTBF calculation
Date and Time of Part Failure	Used to determine Time to Failure for MTBF calculation
Duration of Repair	Used to determine MTTR
Duration of Ramp Down and Ramp Up Time	Used along with Duration of Repair to calculate the business impact of the failure
List of non-failed parts that were replaced during the repair	Used to reset the clock on TTF for the non-failed parts
Number of personnel involved in the repair	Used to help determine the business impact of the failure
Hourly Cost of Downtime	Used to determine the business impact of the failure
Programmatic Information	
Number of RCAs Triggered	Used to calculate RCA completion percentage
Number of RCAs Completed	Used to calculate RCA completion percentage
Number of RCAs Overdue	Used to calculate RCA backlog
Number of Corrective Actions Recommended	Used to calculate Corrective Action Approval Percentage
Number of Corrective Actions Approved	Used to calculate Corrective Action Approval Percentage
Number of Corrective Actions Implemented	Used to calculate Corrective Action Implementation Percentage
Number of Repeat Failures for which Corrective Actions had been implemented	Used to calculate Corrective Action Effectiveness Percentage

3. Determine how data will be collected.

   As you can see in Table 1, there are different types of data that need to be collected. Determining how the data will be collected is an important step that helps determine who will collect the various bits of data required. Failure data can be collected through the EAM/CMMS, automated process data systems, or by using checklists.

Programmatic data may require the use of special forms or special software. End users must make these decisions for themselves. Organizations of different sizes have different capabilities which means what works in one organization may not work in another. The important thing is to make this decision up front and develop the necessary data gathering tools.

4. Determine how data will be analyzed.

Pareto Analysis, Descriptive Statistical Analysis, Weibull Analysis, Root Cause Analysis, RCM Analysis, Simulation and Modeling – which do I choose? The answer is to choose the one or ones that make the most sense in your situation. The best bet is probably to start with Pareto and let it drive where you use other types of analysis to generate corrective actions. Just make sure to remember that data analysis is a tool to help you determine where to apply methods such as RCA and RCM to generate corrective actions. Do not fall victim to analysis paralysis. Analytical reports are nice, but no statistic ever solved a problem.

FRACAS Step 3 – Determine Organizational Roles, Goals, and Responsibilities (RACI)

It is important that everyone in the organization understand their role in the FRACAS process. Some people play very passive roles, while others are very active in the process. Developing the RACI chart is an important step in helping people understand what they are supposed to do.

Seven Steps to a Working FRACAS

Table 10-2: Sample RACI

	Operators	Maintenance Technicians	Ops Supervisors	Maint Supervisors	Ops Manager	Maint Manager	Maint Engineer	Reliability Engineer
Collect Initial Failure Data	R	R	C	C	I	I	R	A
Verify Failure Data			R	R	I	I	R	A
Analyze Failure Data	C	C	C	C	I	I	C	R,A
Manage RCA Program	C	C	C	C	C	C	C	R,A
Collect Programmatic Data	C	C	C	C	I	I	C	R,A
Champion the Program	C	C	C	C	C	C	C	R,A
Monitor Corrective Action Results	R	R	R	R	I	I	R	R,A

Responsible (R) – Those who do the work to achieve the task.

Accountable (A) – The one answerable for the correct and thorough completion of the task, and the one who delegates the work to the responsible person.

Consulted (C) – Those who provide advice and support. Typically subject matter experts.

Informed (I) – Those who are kept up to date on progress.

Responsibility for completion of activities may be shared. Only one person should be accountable for a given activity.

FRACAS Step 4 – Create the FRACAS Policies and Procedures Manual

Once the data collection plan is completed and organizational roles goals and responsibilities have been defined, they should be incorporated into a Policies and Procedures Manual that will serve as the basis for managing and administering the FRACAS system. This is a tedious step, but should not be skipped. It will serve as the basis for developing the initial FRACAS Training Program and for ensuring that new employees receive the information they need to participate effectively in the FRACAS. It is probably best developed as a pocket size book that is easy for people to carry around and refer to as required.

FRACAS

FRACAS Step 5 – Develop and Execute the FRACAS Training Plan

Each person in the organization will need to be trained according to their level of participation in the FRACAS. The first step in developing the Training Plan is to determine which personnel will need what capabilities to successfully carry out their role. A matrix similar to a RACI can be used to perform this step. The roles defined in the RACI are used to determine what capabilities are required.

Table 10-3: Sample Training Matrix

	CMMS Data Entry	Trained?	CMMS Data Extraction	Trained?	Basic Statistical Analysis	Trained?	RCA Facilitator	Trained?	RCA Participant	Trained?	RCM Facilitator	Trained?	RCM Participant	Trained?	Advanced Statistical Analysis	Trained?
Operators	X								X				X			
Maintenance Technicians	X								X				X			
Operations Supervisors	X	Y							X				X			
Maintenance Supervisors	X	Y							X				X			
Operations Manager	X								X				X			
Maintenance Engineer	X		X		X	Y	X		X		X		X			
Reliability Engineer	X		X	Y	X	Y	X	Y	X		X	Y	X		X	

Once you have determined the training requirements, each person should be trained according to the gaps identified in the table. This table will also be used to ensure that newly hired personnel receive the training they need in order to fill their role in the FRACAS process. Make sure you remember to train the Plant Manager.

FRACAS Step 6 – Implement the FRACAS

You have met with management, gained their buy-in, determined the direction you want to go, determined what data you need and how to collect it, and have trained all the right people on what their roles, goals, and responsibilities are. Your next big step is to turn on the FRACAS.

1. Hold required informational meetings.

   It is now time to hold brief informational meetings with everyone to let them know you are ready to begin collecting data and where you intend to start. These meetings should just provide basic information as an introduction and then should be Q&A sessions to help people understand what their roles are. These meetings should not require much time if you have already done a good job of developing and implementing your Training Plan. Most people with key roles will have shared some information with their peers by now.

2. Begin data collection on highest priority systems.

   It is very important to begin collecting data where it will do the most good. Hopefully you have already done criticality analysis and know which systems are creating the majority of facility losses. Start collecting detailed data on those systems so you can best determine the parts that are failing. Remember that it is not systems that fail, but parts that fail. Eliminate the part failures and the system will perform well.

3. Analyze data and report results.

   In a month or so, you will have enough data to start doing some analysis and reporting. You can start looking for common cause failures and common threads in your failures using Pareto Analysis to determine the big hitters. Make sure to analyze data quality as well. Your findings can be reported in the form of graphs and charts on bulletin boards, on your intranet, and through a monthly newsletter/report to key people. Early on, you will be reporting on findings. Within a very short while, you will be able to generate corrective actions based on the Root Cause Analyses that have been done. DO NOT OVERLOOK THE IMPORTANCE OF REPORT-

FRACAS

ING RESULTS. No reporting will soon mean no data gathering by the people responsible for doing it.

4. Create corrective actions based on results.

    Remember, your goal is to eliminate failures. A corrective action is a documented change to either equipment or procedures that has been implemented and verified to be effective. The FRACAS is not just a data collection tool, but rather a system designed to help you create effective corrective actions that eliminate system failures. It is important that this step be done or you will have wasted a lot of time and money only to understand what is causing failures. Focus on results.

FRACAS Step 7 – Monitor and Adjust

1. Monitor data quality and results.

    Good data is the backbone of good decision making. It is important to monitor data quality and make adjustments to either the data collection plan or the training program so that data is consistent and informative. Many organizations believe they have good data only to find out that that can't turn their data into useful information because data collection is inconsistent.

2. Monitor corrective actions.

    It is extremely important to monitor the results of corrective actions to verify their effectiveness. If you hear things like "We have fixed that problem several times in the past few (weeks, months, years)," then your corrective actions have not been very effective.

3. Adjust the data collection plan and the corrective action implementation plan based on results.

    Monitoring the program is important, but only to the extent that it gives you the information you need to generate corrective actions to eliminate FRACAS failures. Remember to document program changes, implement them, and verify that your FRACAS program changes have been effective.

Happy Failure Eliminating!!

ADDENDUM

True Failure Experiences

(All names and data figures have been changed to protect the innocent)

1. FAILURE: Partial Functional Failure Leads to Total Functional Failure

Location: Plant XYZ – Southeast Europe

Basic Cause/Problem:

- Back plate on pump was worn through within two months of installation from new. The product leaking from the casing washed the contaminant from the lubricant and caused catastrophic failure.

Root Cause:

- The rated Q_{min} for the pump is 300 m³/hr, and the actual flow is between 205 m³/hr and 300 m³/hr.
- The pump has been running below its minimum design flow (Q_{min}). Below this flow the impeller was hydraulically imbalanced, causing a low rate of product exchange in the A-cover (back plate opening).
- The silicates (in low concentrations) within the product built up and caused an accelerated level of wear in this chamber. The hydraulic imbalance also caused the high level of vibration at vane pass frequency, which damaged the bearings and dramatically reduced the pump efficiency. The high level of vibration analyst owing to the similarities of the spectrum with hydraulic imbalance. Steps to reduce cavitations were being taken in the

FRACAS

months prior to the failure with no effect and cavitations were only dismissed after observing no pitting damage to the impeller.

Corrective Actions:

1. Reevaluate the correct pump flow requirements.
2. Select and install new pump for new duty, which will be significantly below rating of current pump.
3. Communicate to all plants that the minimum flow-rated flow of pumps should be checked with actual flow when diagnosing vane-pass related problems on centrifugal pumps.
4. Document any partial functional or potential failure in the CMMS/EAM.

2. FAILURE: Gearbox Input Shaft Bearing Failure

Hypothesized Event Sequence

- The bearing inner ring was mounted on a shaft that was machined oversized, outside cylindricity tolerance recommendations and possibly out of round.
- The inner ring would have been seated very tightly over the contact region corresponding to the annular high spot at the off-center position on the shaft seating (cylindricity problem) and more loosely moving axially away from the high spot in both directions.
- These fitting anomalies resulted in an increased tensile hoop stress being exerted on the outer circumferential surface/subsurface of the inner ring. Hoop stress on the inner ring would have been greatest at the region corresponding to the high spot at the off-center position on the shaft seating (cylindricity problem).
- With the bearing in operation under load/misalignment conditions, inner ring stresses would have increased further.

Proposed Event Sequence

- Axial fatigue cracking occurred at a number of locations around the raceway of the inner ring. This cracking would have progressed to a greater magnitude near regions corresponding to the larger diameters caused by any ovality of the shaft bearing seating.

- Fretting corrosion developed between the shaft and inner ring at the interface between the central high spot tight fit and the gradual looser fit moving axially away from the high spot.
- One of the fatigue cracks progressed through approximately 45% of the cross-section of the inner ring before in-service loads caused a final and complete brittle tensile fracture through the remaining section.
- Complete fracture led to a loose inner ring fit on the shaft. The shaft was now free to more easily spin in the ring, causing the 'grinding or machining' - like appearance seen on the inner ring.

Findings/Actions during Stripdown and Rebuild
- The inner ring had rotated on the input shaft damaging this locating diameter.
- The damaged shaft bearing seating was measured at 200.09, center 200.08, then at the other end 200.10mm.
- The undamaged shaft on the inching drive side measured at 200.11mm.
- The gearbox manufacturer recommended that this bearing shaft diameter should have been machined to 200.00+.03mm+.069.
- Both shafts' diameters were reduced to 200.06mm and measured to ensure parallelism within .005mm before fitting of two new SKF C3 clearance bearings.

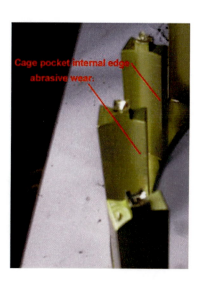

- Cage prong surfaces exhibited no appreciable evidence of wear damage except for the inside edge of a number of the rolling element pockets.
- Suspected that the abrasion of the cage was due to the ingress of steel particles (wear debris) from the fatigue crack.

FRACAS

- The rolling elements were generally in good condition.

- Circumferential wear banding around the rollers was light.

- Rollers exhibited crescent shaped markings around the circumference offset from the central position. Probably damage resulting from the action of the rolling elements passing over the crack sites, especially the advanced crack that led to full fracture.

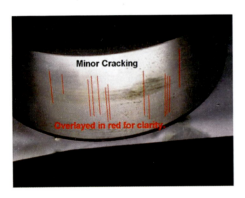

- Large number of secondary crack sites visible on the raceway surface.

Failure Investigation

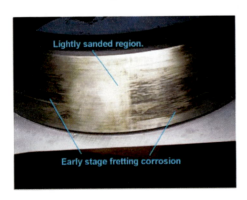

Bearing Designation: NU2240E Manufacturer: FAG

- Fretting corrosion evident on outer surface of bearing outer ring, covering approximately 180, more pronounced over 90.

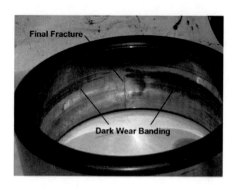

- Inner ring bore marked around the entire circumference with a dark wear band.
- Scoring tended to indicate that inner ring had spun on the shaft. Probable that the ring had spun after the major fracture occurred.
- Thin band suggests that bore of the inner ring was only partially seated on the shaft.

- An inner ring crack extended axially through the entire cross section of the ring.
- The visible fracture surface consistent with fatigue cracking.
- The smoother and more linear crack consistent with fatigue cracking.
- Nature of major crack indicated initiation point at the raceway surface, fatigue caused the crack to propagate through the cross section before final fracture.

Metallurgical Examination

- The inner ring manufactured from standard bearing grade alloy steel (Grade 52100, AS14444-1983). Hardness (nominally 660 HV) as expected for a bearing component.
- Material microstructure examination, particularly around fracture initiation sites, showed no adverse anomalies that could have contributed to crack initiation.
- Major fracture occurred through initial fatigue cracking across approximately 45% of section before final fast fracture across remainder of the section. Mechanism of fatigue cracking was unidirectional alternating bending load. Final fracture from high nominal loading in service.

FRACAS

- Minor cracking was due to alternating bending loads in service.
- The dark wear band seen in the bore appeared to be like that from a machining or grinding process. The area close to the major fracture was damaged to a greater extent in this manner and also showed evidence of fretting corrosion.
- The dark banding was indicative of a small circumferential zone of contact between shaft and bearing bore, the cause which would have been a high spot on the shaft.
- This banding was related to the fatigue cracking. The high spot on the shaft would have caused extreme hoop stresses near the center of the raceway.
- Larger cracks are indicative of higher stress at these points due possibly to an out-of-round shaft.

Conclusions
- Failure of the FAG NU2240E CRB gearbox high-speed input shaft was a result of improper machining and fitting tolerances on the shaft bearing seating.
- The major contributing factors were the mounting of the bearing on a shaft that was oversized, outside cylindricity tolerance recommendation, and possibly out of round.
- These factors contributed to an increase in inner ring hoop stress that was aggravated during operation by abnormal radial load induced by misalignment.
- Failure was through fracture of the inner ring due to the action of fatigue stress-related cracking,ess load.
- The shaft was operating at 990rpm, which is around half of the speed rating for this bearing operating in oil lubrication. This would discount one other possible source of increased hoop stress being applied to the inner ring, that being through the action of centrifugal inertia forces that would be generated at excessively high bearing operating speed.
- During repair to the gearbox, the shaft bearing seating diameter was reduced to 200.06mm, putting diametral tolerance at the upper end of an n6 tolerance.
- Measured the tolerance on cylindricity at $5\mu m$, which is within recommended standard.

Addendum

Help Documents

Accurate Work Order Close Out
"TOOL BOX TRAINING"
Reference: ISO 14224

Accurate Work Order Close Out is important for the continuous improvement of any organization.

The objective of accurate data collection is to assist management in making the right decisions at the right time and to empower workers to make decisions at the floor level.

General Rules:

Work Orders should have the following, at minimum:

1. All work is covered by a work order.
2. The correct Work Order code (breakdown (1), urgent (2), etc.).
3. The correct equipment number, at the right level.
4. The maintenance person's accurate total work hours charged to this work order.
5. The start time and completed time on the job.
6. Comments from the maintenance person as to what work was performed.
7. Any recommendation to changes to maintenance strategy or procedure.
8. Any parts used whether from the storeroom or not.
9. The maintenance person's signature.

WARNING: Without the above information, one cannot determine:

- Actual maintenance cost for specific assets
- Mean Time Between Failure
- Mean Time To Repair
- Mean Time Between Repairs
- Rework
- If a PM Procedure is effective

FRACAS

- If a specific type repair is effective
- If a maintenance strategy meets the intent of the end users

10. Repair or Corrective Work orders must include everything as stated above plus:
    a. Component code
    b. Failure code
    c. Cause code

11. Without the previously stated information, one cannot determine the:
    a. **Dominant Failure Thread** – which component has the most specific failure modes with a specific cause across multiple assets.

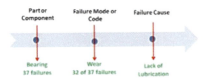

   b. **Dominant Failure Pattern** – which failure pattern is the most dominant, and what are the major causes of failures for this pattern. This allows one to develop strategies to eliminate unacceptable failures which impact the organization.

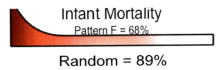

WARNING: Without the above information one cannot determine:
   a. The **Component** (across area, plant, etc) with the most failures.
   b. The most frequent **Failure Mode** for the most frequently failed component.
   c. The Component **"Cause"** for the majority of these failures.
   d. **Pareto Causes of Failures** in most **"Dominant Failure Pattern."**

"In the absence of quality data, we have reactivity" - **Just a thought!**

Key Definitions

Crisis failures: failures that are highly visible, and can be handled by a singular type of report such as an incident report that captures the basic elements of the incident.

Corrective Action: A [documented and validated] change in the design of a system, product, or process (including software-related designs) that is intended to reduce the rate of occurrence of failure modes.

Defect: an abnormality in a part which leads to equipment or asset failure if not corrected in time.

Failure: an unsatisfactory condition. In other words, a failure is an identifiable deviation from the original condition which is unsatisfactory to a particular user.

Failure Codes Creation: The Failure Codes (Defect) in a Computerized Maintenance Management System (CMMS) should match very closely, if not verbatim, to the failure modes listed in the failure modes library. These failure codes must address specific failure codes for specific components. Do not use a general library of failure codes.

Failure Mode: how something fails.

Failure Modes Analysis: the block that represents the entire EMP Analysis and all of the known failure modes that are expected to occur.

Functional Failure: the inability of an item (or the equipment containing it) to meet a specified performance standard. It is usually identified by an operator.

Hidden Failures: functional failures that share two very important characteristics: First, they can't be seen by the operators during normal operation of the system. Second, they are usually in items that protect people from severe injury or death, or protect equipment from severe damage.

Maintenance: to maintain or keep in an existing condition; to keep, preserve, protect.

FRACAS

Potential Failure: an identifiable physical condition which indicates a functional failure is imminent and is usually identified by a maintenance technician using Predictive or quantitative Preventive Maintenance.

P-F Curve: illustrates the timing of when a defect begins. Once it is detected the point on the PF curve is point "P." If the defect is detected early enough and repaired properly, reliability is restored. If the defect is not repaired it will result in catastrophic failure which is point "F" on the P-F curve.

On the P-F curve shown in Figure A you can see how the defect severity increases from low to critical over time if not corrected.

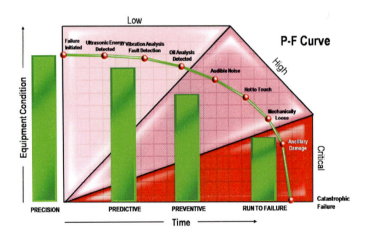

Figure A: PF Curve

RACI Charting: a technique for identifying functional areas, key activities, and decision points where ambiguities exist. With RACI, differences can be brought into the open and resolved through a team effort.

RACI Chart - Preventive and Predictive Maintenance Effectiveness

Decisions / Functions	Maint. Manager	Plant Manager	Maint. Supervisor	Maint. Tech	Production Mgr	Reliability Engr	Planner/Scheduler
Is the Plant running at a high reliability rate?	R	A	I	I	C	C	I
Was the PM/PdM program developed based on Failure Modes?	A	I/R	I/R	R	C/R	R	R
Does the plant have a measure system in place to measure health of the assets?	R	A	I	I	C	R	I

"R"	Responsible	"the doer"
"A"	Accountable	"the buck stops here"
"C"	Consult	"in the loop"
"I"	Inform	"keep in the picture"

Reliability: the ability of a system or component to perform its required functions under stated conditions for a specified period of time.

Reliability Centered Maintenance (RCM): a process to ensure that assets continue to do what their users require in their present operating context.

Seven Questions of RCM:

1. What is the item supposed to do, and what are its associated performance standards?
2. In what ways can it fail to provide the required functions?
3. What are the events that cause each failure?
4. What happens when each failure occurs?
5. In what way does each failure matter?
6. What systematic task can be performed proactively to prevent, or to diminish to a satisfactory degree, the consequences of the failure?
7. What must be done if a suitable preventive task cannot be found?

Strategy: development of a prescriptive plan toward a specific goal.

FRACAS

Failure Collection Series

Tube Corrosion   **New Gear – Old Gear**

Boiler Tube Failure   **Bearing Failure**

Results from Coupling Failure   **Lubrication Failure - Large Gearbox**

Pipe Failure Resulted in a Major Leak

Motor Winding Failure

Motor Coupling Failure

Worn Sprocket with New Chain?

Spalling, Heavy Loading on One Side

Shaft Not Sized to Fit Coupling

Potential Failures

Potential Failure: an identifiable physical condition which indicates a functional failure is imminent and is usually identified by a maintenance technician using Predictive or quantitative Preventive maintenance

Defect: an abnormality in a part which leads to equipment or asset failure if not corrected in time

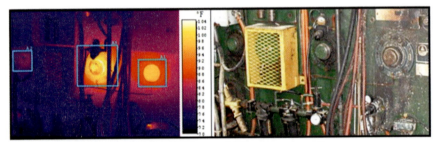

Bearing Defects – Infrared Thermography

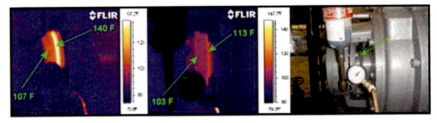

Seal Defect - Infrared Thermography

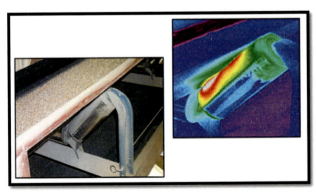

Conveyor Roller Defect - Infrared Thermography

Addendum

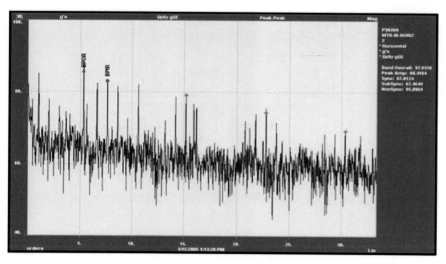

Bearing Defect – Ultrasound Technology

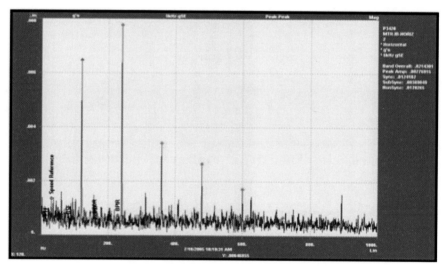

Rotor Bar Defect – Ultrasound Technology

FRACAS

Adhesive Wear – Oil Analysis

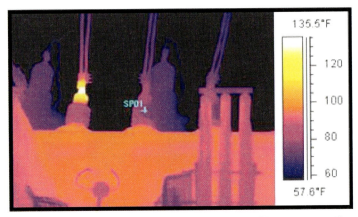

Electrical Insulator Defect - Infrared Thermography

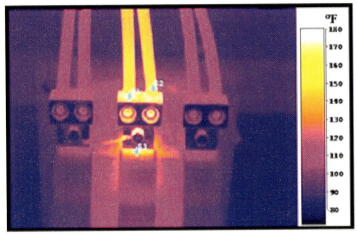

Electrical Defect - Infrared Thermography
(further investigation required)

Addendum

High Voltage Connection Defect – Infrared Thermography

133

About the Authors

Ricky Smith, CMRP, CPMM
Senior Technical Director

Ricky has over 30 years experience in maintenance as a maintenance manager, maintenance supervisor, maintenance engineer, maintenance training specialist, maintenance consultant and is a well known published author. Today he is a Senior Technical Advisor for GP*Allied*. Ricky has worked with maintenance organizations in hundreds of facilities, industrial plants, etc, world wide in developing reliability, maintenance and technical training strategies.

Prior to joining Allied Reliability in 2008, Ricky worked as a professional maintenance employee for Exxon Company USA, Alumax (this plant was rated the best in the world for over 18 years), Kendall Company, and Hercules Chemical providing the foundation for his reliability and maintenance experience.

Ricky is the Vice Chairman of the Society for Maintenance and Reliability Professionals Oil and Gas Special Interest Group and the Reliability Engineering Discipline Manager for PetroSkills.

Ricky is the co-author of "Rules of Thumb for Maintenance and Reliability Engineers", "Lean Maintenance" and "Industrial Repair, Best Maintenance Repair Practices", "Planning and Scheduling Made Simple". Ricky also writes for different magazines during the past 20 years on technical, reliability and maintenance subjects.

Ricky holds certification as Certified Maintenance and Reliability Professional (CMRP) from the Society for Maintenance and Reliability Professionals (SMRP) as well as a Certified Plant Maintenance Manager (CPMM) from the Association of Facilities Engineering (AFE).

Ricky lives in Charleston, SC with his wife. Aside form spending time with his 3 children and 3 grandchildren, Ricky enjoys kayaking, fishing, hiking and archaeology.

Bill Keeter, CMRP
Senior Technical Advisor

Bill has been implementing equipment performance improvement programs since the late 1970's when he was the motor officer for a newly activated field artillery battalion. The unit was activated using surplus Korean War era equipment that was proving to be difficult to maintain and operate. Under his guidance the battalion implemented a comprehensive and effective equipment maintenance plan that resulted in zero equipment failures during extensive field exercises.

As a maintenance manager in the late 1990's, Bill led his maintenance team through a very successful reliability improvement effort at a plastic film manufacturing plant. They were able to improve equipment availability from the low 80% range to the upper 90% range within a two year period of time by implementing a comprehensive condition monitoring program, creating a culture of "why", and emphasizing the importance of the involvement of every team member in the reliability and planning effort.

Bill has been providing consulting and training for reliability improvement efforts in a wide variety of industries since 2001. During that time he has used analytical methods such as Reliability-Centered Maintenance (RCM), Root Cause Analysis (RCA), Reliability, Availability, Maintainability, and Safety Modeling (RAMS), and Life-Cycle Cost Analysis (LCCA) to analyze failures, develop equipment maintenance plans, and improve system performance. Bill became interested in FRACAS when he found that most companies he worked with did not have the detailed data they needed to make the analyses as accurate as they could be. Few if any organizations were documenting which parts were failing and causing functional failures in their systems.

About Reliabilityweb.com

Created in 1999, Reliabilityweb.com provides educational information and peer-to-peer networking opportunities that enable safe and effective maintenance reliability and asset management for organizations around the world.
Activities include:

Reliabilityweb.com (www.reliabilityweb.com) includes educational articles, tips, video presentations, an industry event calendar and industry news. Updates are available through free email subscriptions and RSS feeds. **Confiabilidad.net** is a mirror site that is available in Spanish at www.confiabilidad.net

Uptime Magazine (www.uptimemagazine.com) is a bi-monthly magazine launched in 2005 that is highly prized by the maintenance reliability and asset management community. Editions are obtainable in print, online, digital, Kindle and through the iPad/iPhone app.

Reliability Performance Institute Conferences and Training Events (www.maintenanceconference.com) offer events that range from unique, focused-training workshops and seminars to small focused conferences to large industry-wide events, including the International Maintenance Conference, RELIABILITY 2.0 and Solutions 2.0.

MRO-Zone Bookstore (www.mro-zone.com) is an online bookstore offering a maintenance reliability and asset management focused library of books, DVDs and CDs published by Reliabilityweb.com.

Association for Maintenance Professionals (www.maintenance.org) is a member organization and online community that encourages professional development and certification and supports information exchange and learning with 10,000+ members worldwide.

A Word About Social Good

Reliabilityweb.com is mission driven to deliver value and social good to the maintenance reliability and asset management communities. *Doing good work and making profit is not inconsistent*, and as a result of Reliabilityweb.com's mission-driven focus, financial stability and success has been the outcome. For over a decade, Reliabilityweb.com's positive contributions and commitment to the maintenance reliability and asset management communities have been unmatched.

Other Causes

Reliabilityweb.com has financially contributed to include industry associations, such as SMRP, AFE, STLE, ASME and ASTM, and community charities, including the Salvation Army, American Red Cross, Wounded Warrior Project, Paralyzed Veterans of America and the Autism Society of America. In addition, we are proud supporters of our U.S. Troops and first responders who protect our freedoms and way of life. That is only possible by being a for-profit company that pays taxes.

I hope you will get involved with and explore the many resources that are available to you through the Reliabilityweb.com network.

Warmest regards,
Terrence O'Hanlon
CEO, Reliabilityweb.com